Assessing Learning in the Primary Classroom

Sandra Johnson

Routledge
Taylor & Francis Group

LONDON AND NEW YORK

First published 2012
by Routledge
2 Park Square, Milton Park, Abingdon, Oxon OX14 4RN

Simultaneously published in the USA and Canada
by Routledge
711 Third Avenue, New York, NY 10017

Routledge is an imprint of the Taylor & Francis Group, an informa business

British Library Cataloguing in Publication Data
A catalogue record for this book is available from the British Library

Library of Congress Cataloging in Publication Data
Johnson, Sandra, 1946–
Assessing learning in the primary classroom / Sandra Johnson
    p. cm. -- (Understanding primary education series)
    372. Educational tests and measurements--Great Britain. 2. Educational evaluation--
Great Britain. 3. Education (Elementary)--Great Britain. I. Title
LB3056.G7J55 2012   372.41-dc23
2011022534

ISBN: 978-0-415-56275-1 (hbk)
ISBN: 978-0-415-56276-8 (pbk)
ISBN: 978-0-203-15500-4 (ebk)

Typeset in Gill Sans and Times New Roman
by Bookcraft Ltd, Stroud, Gloucestershire

MIX
Paper from
responsible sources
FSC® C004839
www.fsc.org

Printed and bound in Great Britain by
TJ International Ltd, Padstow, Cornwall

Contents

List of figures

List of tables

Series editor's preface

When you sit with a child in your class, talk to them, and help them learn, you have built on one of the most important abilities of a good teacher: the ability to assess. Your understanding of that pupil's needs built up over the year, your aims for the activity they are carrying out, your reading of their work, your observation of them while carrying out an activity, and your ability to see learning as a complex developmental process, have all been utilised to support the child's learning. At the heart of Sandra Johnson's book is an exploration of the knowledge and understanding that teachers need in order to assess their pupils effectively. The book also shares an appreciation of the powerful importance of assessment at different levels, and in a range of contexts, to help the development of teachers' *assessment literacy*.

If there is one single thing that has dominated education in England since 1988 it is assessment. In 2011 the Conservative/Liberal Democrat government based its rationale for the review of the National Curriculum in England on the claim that England's standing in assessments internationally had declined. The government also introduced a phonics test for all six-year-old children, in spite of two-thirds of respondents to the consultation not supporting such a move. As Sandra Johnson points out in the chapter on statutory assessment:

> While the government has confirmed, in response to consultation, that school by school results will not be published, it has nevertheless also confirmed that schools' results, counter to the overwhelmingly negative view of the 1000+ responses to the 2011 consultation, will be required to be submitted centrally for use by other educational professionals 'to drive good quality systematic teaching of phonics in schools' (DfE 2011: 9). National, regional and local authority statistics will be published, even though over 70 per cent of consultation respondents were against this.

These significant events in 2011 can be seen as part of a trajectory of increasing reliance on formal testing that began in 1988. In spite of significant resistance to statutory testing by large numbers of people in England, successive governments have continued to increase their control over education through testing, targets and league tables of performance. Yet on England's doorstep the countries of Scotland, Wales and Northern Ireland have pursued very different policies, as this book reveals. The approach to statutory assessment in England has had a direct influence on the curriculum and pedagogy, areas that in the past were deemed to be the domain of teachers and pupils. In view of the continued use and misuse of assessment, its high stakes nature, and its impact on teachers and pupils, this book could not be more timely or more necessary. If teachers are to fight for the most appropriate education for their pupils they need the kind of assessment literacy that this book offers.

Sandra Johnson brings her wealth of experience and expertise to shed light on everything from the design of assessment tasks to the ways that international comparisons work. A range of topics from the straightforward to the complex are explained with clarity and incisiveness. I know that teachers and educationalists at all levels of experience will enjoy reading this book, and I hope, armed with the knowledge the book imparts, will be emboldened to challenge inappropriate policy and practice.

Dominic Wyse, Senior Lecturer in Primary and Early Years Education,
Cambridge University, UK
June 2011

Acknowledgements

First and foremost, I thank both Wynne Harlen and Dominic Wyse for giving me the opportunity to write this book, and for having confidence in my ability to do it. Thanks also to Jannette Elwood for the information about assessment in Northern Ireland that is included in Chapter 6. I owe a debt of gratitude to Linda Owens and Catherine Waldron for their vital practitioner feedback on early chapter drafts, some of which they read and commented on more than once. Finally, my husband, Rod Johnson, deserves special mention, not only for his patience, encouragement and support throughout the writing process, and for his extensive proofreading and consequent stylistic improvements, but also for all of those times that he helped me to structure my thoughts when inspiration failed and commitment threatened to vaporise.

Chapter 1

Introduction

What is 'assessment', and why is assessment so important in the teaching–learning process? What is 'assessment literacy', and why is it essential for any education professional working in primary education to be assessment literate? Chapter 1 raises these and other questions, setting the scene for the book as a whole. Four groups of professionals are identified for whom assessment literacy is essential in order to carry out their responsibilities competently. These are class teachers, assessment coordinators, headteachers and local authority subject advisers. Brief examples are offered to illustrate how essential it is for these individuals to be assessment literate, and it is the needs of these groups in particular that feature throughout the following chapters.

Why is assessment important?

Assessment is an essential and integral component in the teaching and learning process, for evaluating how effectively teachers are teaching and pupils are learning. The results of assessment are also a critical ingredient in the process of school and system evaluation, and in the evaluation of new curriculum initiatives and delivery strategies. 'Assessment literacy' is a term you may have heard often recently. It simply means being familiar with the fundamental concepts of educational assessment, so that you can not only assess confidently and competently yourself but also be in a position to evaluate the quality of others' assessments. Every education professional needs to be assessment literate. And assessment literacy is what this book is about.

Teachers need to engage in a variety of forms of assessment throughout their teaching–learning activity, so that they can monitor and evaluate their students' learning, and make appropriate adjustments to their lesson planning in light of their findings. You might have come across the term 'assessment for learning', or 'formative assessment', which describes this ongoing, integrated, interactive, informal, in-class assessment. Teachers are also typically required to assess in some meaningful summarised form the final outcomes of their teaching, in terms of their pupils' achievements and current state of learning development, for the benefit of parents and other teachers. This is often referred to as 'assessment *of* learning', or 'summative assessment'. But don't let these different terms confuse you. They all concern the same activity of assessing pupils' learning. Assessment *for* learning is in principle the same thing as assessment *of* learning. What differs is the use made of the assessment results, which sometimes demands differences in the ways in which you assess and in how often you assess.

Assessment can take many different forms. The process of assessment can consume greater or lesser amounts of time and effort, and impose different degrees of burden on teachers and students, depending on what is being assessed and why. As a class teacher you will be directly involved in assessing your pupils' learning progress and final achievements. As an assessment coordinator you will constantly be evaluating your school's assessment policies and practices, and suggesting improvements as appropriate. As a headteacher you will find yourself reviewing the results of your teachers' assessments, as well as those of other similar schools, as one aspect of your school's self-evaluation. And wherever you are in the school system, you will, from time to time, need, or want, to evaluate claims made for the superiority of one teaching strategy or curriculum design over another. Typically this will require you to evaluate the results of pupil assessment in addition to other aspects of comparative studies. Consider, for instance, the following examples of education professionals assessing or simply using assessment results in their work. Imagine yourself in their shoes, and reflect on how assessment literate you would need to be to perform each role well.

Example 1: Class teacher as assessor

You are in your first post as a class teacher, working in a small primary school in a pleasant rural village. You have been assigned to Year 3, and you have 29 pupils in your class. While you will be expected to teach the various topics in the subjects of the National Curriculum, you will have some flexibility in how and when you teach them. You will need to devise your own programme of work for the term and for the year, and to prepare your lesson plans. This will not be a problem for you, since you had quite a bit of practice doing this in your initial teacher training course. So you will be quite confident about that part of your job. However, you also know that you will be expected to monitor your pupils' learning in the various subjects over the year, and that you will need to be prepared to submit meaningful reports on their progress to parents and to your headteacher from time to time. You feel less confident about this aspect of your work, because you had rather little guidance on assessment during your initial training. So where do you start? When should you begin assessing your pupils, and how? How will you know that your assessment strategies are appropriate and that your assessment results are trustworthy? You know that formative assessment is considered an essential element, to be integrated into the teaching–learning interaction that you have day-to-day with your pupils. But what does this mean in practice? Where do you begin?

Example 2: Teacher as assessment coordinator

There is so much external assessment, as well as internal assessment, now going on in primary schools that most schools have identified one teacher as 'assessment coordinator' or 'assessment leader'. You have been working for three years in a medium-sized school in a large city environment, and your head has just invited you to become your school's assessment leader. You will be responsible for coordinating all the assessment activity in your school. Among your many tasks will be ensuring that statutory assessments are carried out properly and on time, that any pretesting that your school has agreed to undertake for test-development agencies is organised as instructed, and that if your school is selected at random for participation in a national or international attainment survey the appropriate pupils are tested under standardised conditions at the appropriate times. And you will further be responsible for delivering the results of all of this testing to the relevant individuals and organisations. In addition, you will be expected to keep up-to-date on assessment developments as these concern primary education, including new teaching approaches and commercial tests. What skills and knowledge will you need to meet this responsibility efficiently? Most importantly, how confident will you be about advising your headteacher on how your school's assessment policies might be evaluated and, if necessary, improved?

Example 3: Headteacher as school manager

Imagine now that you are the headteacher of a medium-sized primary school in a large market town. You have around 350 pupils in your school, with two parallel classes in every year. Your school is fed by a handful of preschool centres and itself feeds into a large comprehensive school on the outskirts of the town. You have an active and committed Board of Governors, an equally interested and supportive parent group, and, of course, you liaise regularly with the senior staff in your local education authority. Your school also hosts inspectors from time to time, and you are due for a comprehensive inspection within the next three months. As head you are responsible for all aspects of school management and functioning, from building maintenance to health and safety issues to pupil attainment outcomes. Most importantly in this context, your job implicitly involves you in school self-evaluation, and much of the information you will be using as a basis for this will be assessment results of various kinds. If your evaluations are to be soundly based you will need to feel very comfortable handling numbers. But equally importantly you will need to have the skills and knowledge to be able to evaluate the quality of the assessment results you are reviewing, and indeed to evaluate, and if necessary to challenge, the conclusions of your school's inspection report. Do you have the relevant skills?

Example 4: Local authority adviser as programme evaluator

You took up your current post as a local authority adviser a couple of years ago, with particular responsibility for language and literacy. You feel fairly comfortable in the role now, having faced quite a few new challenges at first. Like any primary adviser you liaise with all the primary schools in your authority, supporting their provision by keeping them up-to-date with relevant subject developments and resource availability. In addition, you are a conduit for the sharing of expertise and good practice among the schools themselves. New curricula, new teaching approaches and new assessment tools and practices are all within your general remit. When a new language teaching programme is announced, or a new reading test published, you need to know about it, study it and decide whether or not to recommend it for adoption in your own authority. So when you hear excited talk about the effectiveness of a new scheme for teaching beginning reading, 'synthetic phonics' is a topical example, you will want to evaluate for yourself the evidence on which the claims for superiority are based. What kind of evidence would you be looking for? Where would you look for it? What questions would you ask to help you to come to a view about the validity of the 'evidence' that is offered? How confident are you that you could carry out a professional evaluation?

The nature of assessment

Educational assessment is essentially to do with gathering evidence about what pupils know, understand, think and can do, with some particular purpose in mind. We can assess knowledge, skills and attitudes informally, through interaction, observation and questioning over some more or less lengthy period of time, or formally, through use of structured interviews, tasks, tests and questionnaires. And pupils can assess themselves, or be assessed by others, including their peers, teachers and external agencies. But what evidence do we look for when we assess pupils? When and where do we look for it? How exactly should we gather it, and how will we know when we have enough? The answers to these questions depend very much on the nature of what is being assessed, what the context for assessment is, who is doing the assessment, and why it is being carried out.

Assessment is not always an easy task. This is especially so when we are trying to assess intellectual abilities and skills, opinions and attitudes. Why? Partly because what we want to assess is often difficult to define clearly. But, equally importantly, however well we succeed in defining it, unlike, say, height or weight, the 'it' cannot always be directly observed, least of all directly measured. Because of this, we have to employ a variety of strategies in order to gather relevant evidence on which to base our assessment. We ask pupils questions, and reflect on their responses. Or we give them instructions to do something, and we observe their behaviour as they carry out the task.

The 'assessment instrument' might be an informal task-based exercise conducted during normal class time. The task could be to produce a piece of creative writing, about a visiting alien maybe, to collaborate in a small group exercise, for example to produce a poster about climate change, or to keep a record of playground temperatures. Then again, the assessment instrument might be a teacher-made pencil-and-paper test, comprising a number of simple fraction problems perhaps. Or it might be a commercial standardised reading test. Or it could be a questionnaire, in which you include a number of questions about your pupils' reading habits, and likes and dislikes, in order to assess their levels of learning motivation. Not forgetting all the possibilities for pupil assessment that you can find in any interactive discussion with your pupils.

You might mark or rate the outcomes of your questions, tests and tasks – the pupils' answers, their behaviours and the products they create – and, where relevant, summarise them in some way, typically as total or average test scores. These might lead to immediate decisions about your pupils. Examples would include end-of-term 'reading ages' based on use of a standardised reading test, classifications into 'performance percentiles' for the class or entire school, based on the results of a science investigation, or an attainment-level decision based on performances in National Curriculum mathematics assessments. Alternatively, the assessment result could simply be recorded for use later, perhaps for contribution to a portfolio, or to add to the results of a series of other assessments held over the year, whose combined results might be summarised to furnish the basis for an evaluative decision about achievement, progress and future placement.

In principle, assessment can appear to be quite a simple exercise, and sometimes it is. But numerous extraneous influences can affect the process, introducing potential inconsistency and 'noise' into the results. Assessing subject knowledge is already a difficult exercise. You can ask a pupil to tell you the date of some famous battle in English history. You can ask for the name of the general in charge of the battle. You can ask how many soldiers died. And so on. Some pupils will answer all three questions correctly or all three incorrectly. Others might answer one or two correctly and the third not. You might ask other questions on the same general theme. But what would the outcome of the questioning tell us about the pupil's historical knowledge? If we added some questions that required the pupil to reason about events, perhaps to explain why this or that strategy was adopted by the commanding officer, we might change the picture. If we had asked the same questions the day before, or the day after, or the following week, would the outcome have been the same, for every individual pupil? What difference would it have made had you explored your pupils' knowledge in some other way?

Skills assessment can be more straightforward, or equally challenging, depending on the nature of the skills concerned. For example, if you want to know whether a pupil can weigh three grams of flour you can simply ask the pupil to do that and judge accordingly. But in real life this would typically be just one small task within a longer exercise, baking a cake for example. How would you assess the pupil's performance on the whole task? You might devise a checklist, and note which of various steps the pupil completes adequately according to your assessment criteria. But if not all the steps are completed correctly how would you use the overall profile of successes and failures to come to a decision about the pupil's cake-making skills? And how far could you generalise this one result to the pupil's 'cookery skills'? How confident could you be that the generalisation is defensible?

Coverage and objectives of this book

This book focuses on four fundamental questions:

1   What is assessment?
2   How do you assess pupil learning?
3   What purposes do assessment results serve?
4   What criteria should you use to judge the quality of assessment results?

We have addressed the first question to some extent here, in Chapter 1. But you will learn more about the nature of assessment in the following chapters.

Chapters 2, 3 and 4 are principally concerned with the second and third questions, about how and why we assess. Various ways in which we can assess learning in and outside the classroom are described in Chapter 2, which also explores the question of how you might integrate assessment into your regular classroom activity. In particular you will learn more about formative assessment, and how this is expected to improve learning, about summative assessment, which summarises a pupil's current achievements, and about diagnostic assessment. The chapter touches on the challenging question of assessment record keeping in the primary classroom.

Chapter 3 overviews all the different types of question, item and task that we can choose among when we assess pupils. 'Constructed response' item formats, 'select' item formats, and 'performance assessment' tasks are covered in this chapter. Chapter 4 focuses on how we make appropriate item and task choices to create tests. The chapter begins by considering the first step in planning and creating assessments, which is developing assessment objectives. The objectives are then operationalised through the creation of appropriate assessment tools, i.e. tests, practical tasks, checklists, and so on. 'Norm-referencing', 'criterion-referencing', 'targeted testing' are among the terms explained in this chapter.

Chapter 5 addresses the fourth question, about judging assessment quality, where quality is a combination of assessment 'validity' and the often quite neglected, but essential, quality component that is 'reliability'. These very important assessment concepts are fully explained.

Chapters 6 and 7 turn to question 3, looking in particular at two of the important accountability purposes of assessment. Chapter 6 is devoted to statutory assessment, principally with respect to England, but with a brief overview of the situation in the other countries of the UK. National Curriculum assessment evolved in important ways almost from its inception, and is evolving still. The chapter describes the current assessment requirements for primary schools, adopting a critical approach to this initiative and inviting you to evaluate the state of play at this point in time. Statutory assessment in the Early Years Foundation Stage is also overviewed, as is the imminent statutory use of a 'phonic check' for six-year-olds.

Chapter 7 looks at system evaluation, and in particular at how large-scale assessment surveys are used to judge the effectiveness of national educational systems, either by comparing attainment outcomes against a set of domestic criteria or against pupil perform-ance in other countries. The chapter begins with an historical overview of the kinds of system-wide assessment strategies that have been implemented in the UK over the last 60 years or so, culminating in the picture as we know it today. The chapter moves on to consider the international survey programmes organised by the International Association for the Evaluation of Educational Achievement (IEA), that directly concern primary education, and the Organisation for Economic Cooperation and Development (OECD), whose Programme for International Student Assessment (PISA) was launched just over a decade ago. The PISA programme focuses on 15-year-olds, but is included here because of its growing impact on educational policy worldwide. PISA's policy impact extends to primary education as well as secondary education, and so should be of interest to all education professionals, in whichever sector they work.

Chapter 8 focuses on how the different kinds of assessment information are typically used in evaluation activity of different kinds by different types of education professional, from class teachers to headteachers, from authority advisers to school inspectors, from civil serv-ants to education directors and ministers. Pupil evaluation, teacher evaluation, school evalu-ation, system evaluation and programme evaluation are all discussed, as is the vital need for individuals engaged in these various activities to be assessment literate.

Chapter 2

Accessing and using evidence
of learning

Why do we assess pupil learning? How can we assess whether pupils have remembered a fact, understood a concept, developed an attitude, or acquired a skill that we have tried to transmit to them, to teach them, in our classrooms? What is the meaning of 'formative assessment', 'summative assessment' and 'diagnostic assessment'? How detailed do your assessment records have to be? These are the principal questions addressed in Chapter 2, which looks at:

- Purposes of assessment
- Gathering assessment evidence in the classroom
- Formative, summative and diagnostic assessment
- Record keeping.

Purposes of assessment

Why do we assess pupil learning? This is an important question whose answer will be obvious to some but perhaps less so to others. There are two primary purposes for assessing pupils: 'to inform decisions about learning experiences and to report on what has been achieved' (Harlen 2007: 15). But there can be many secondary purposes, in terms of the uses that are made of assessment results.

Within the classroom, we assess learning because we need to know how *well* pupils are learning, individually and as a group, in order to monitor and, if necessary, improve our own effectiveness as teachers. If taught facts are not being memorised by pupils, if skills are not being securely acquired, if concepts are not being fully understood, then we would want to address these problems as soon as possible before moving on to further work that builds on prior learning. This might mean revising lesson plans to make space to reteach a fact, skill or concept, to an individual child, to a group of children or to the whole class. Curriculum-embedded assessment will not only benefit current pupils in their learning, facilitating more effective learning through frequent and constructive feedback from you on their achievements, but will also help you to evaluate your own effectiveness as a teacher.

In addition to benefits for our pupils and for ourselves as teachers, we also need to assess learning so that others might be informed about learning progress and achievement. 'Others' will include parents, who have a natural interest in and concern for how well their children are benefiting from their education. Also included here are other teachers in the school, some of whom will not only be interested in but will need to know 'where your pupils are' at particular points, especially should they be about to take over the job of teaching from you as the children move up to the next class. And, of course, the headteacher will need to be kept informed about the progress children in the school are making in their learning, so that this critical information can feed into the school's ongoing process of self-evaluation (this is discussed further in Chapters 7 and 8). Let us not forget also the school governors, who will be keen to see the outcomes of the school's self-evaluation reports, given their statutory responsibility to support the school in overcoming any perceived weaknesses.

At any stage of schooling, but better earlier than later, children with emerging learning difficulties will need to be assessed in order to diagnose any physical, physiological and psychological reasons for their learning problems. Armed with this information, we can design individualised learning programmes for such children, and make arrangements to provide them with appropriate types of additional support during assessment.

Beyond the school itself we can mention the interests of teachers in other schools that a pupil in your class might be transferred to at any point, because of family relocations, bullying problems, and so on. Then there are headteachers in other schools of similar type, who will want to compare your school's achievement outcomes with their own. The local authority will have an official interest, as it engages in its own system evaluation activity. So, too, will school inspectors, who act for the government in monitoring standards in individual schools, and who regularly conduct broad-ranging evaluations of schools, covering a variety of aspects including pupil attainment. Finally, there is the government itself, which needs assessment information with which to address its system evaluation responsibilities, an aspect discussed in Chapter 7.

Assessment results can be used for class placement within secondary schools and larger primary schools, and for selection into some secondary schools. Assessment results in the lower secondary school will also help determine which subjects pupils will continue to study for later external examinations and at what levels.

To summarise, assessment in the primary school is necessary:

- to inform pupils about their learning, so that they and their teachers can take immediate action to build on strengths and address any weaknesses
- to provide teachers with information for self-evaluation
- to diagnose any medical or psychological problems that a child might have that impedes learning, so that appropriate help and support might be organised
- to provide other teachers with information about pupils' achievements, especially at the stage of transfer to another class or to another school
- to inform parents about the progress of their children
- to provide headteachers with information about pupils' achievements, to feed into school self-evaluation and to be available to school governors and inspectors
- to meet statutory assessment requirements.

There are many motivations for assessment, and the list above is not exhaustive. Newton (2010) provides a more comprehensive account of ways in which assessment results are used within and outside schools, at different stages in the educational system. You will also find a stimulating overview of the many purposes of assessment in Mansell *et al.* (2009), along with a critical reflection on how well different kinds of assessment can be expected to meet different needs.

Your principal responsibility as a primary class teacher is to ensure that the assessments that you make of your pupils are 'fit for purpose', whatever the given purposes that you are aware of might be. But how should you go about assessing your pupils? Do you need to make your own tests? Do you have to use commercial tests chosen by your school's assessment coordinator? Are there other ways to assess learning that do not involve tests? Are you *obliged* to use any or all of these?

The next section focuses on how you can use numerous opportunities during your regular teaching and learning interaction in the classroom to assess your pupils, individually and in groups, so that you build up a store of assessment evidence in an informal way, to use immediately or later to meet the different assessment demands that are made of you.

Gathering assessment evidence in the classroom

How can we assess whether pupils have remembered a fact, understood a concept, developed an attitude, or acquired a skill that we have tried to transmit to them, to teach them, in our classrooms? This is a critical question for any teacher, given the importance of periodically checking on learning, continually monitoring progress, and summarising a child's state of achievement at particular points for particular audiences.

In practice it is usually relatively easy to find out what young children know, think and can do, at least in specific terms. Pupils are often willing participants in classroom interaction, especially with their teachers. And arguably the most common and the quickest ways to assess learning are to question, to discuss and to observe. We ask our pupils questions, orally or on paper, individually or within a group, formally or informally. And usually we get answers, which, right or wrong, provide us with evidence of successful learning or of persisting learning needs. We can also observe children, in individual or group activities, including discussions, at any point in their schooling. We can have them draw, write, discuss, present, sing, dance, create concept maps, and so on, and through observation and questions check on their learning and progress in terms of our learning objectives for those activities.

Take, for example, a typical early reception class activity, which takes as its focus a familiar rhyming song like 'Ten green bottles'. The song itself is just four lines long, but it is sung over and over again. The first verse refers to ten green bottles, of which one breaks, leaving nine. The next verse repeats the lyrics but this time with nine bottles in place of ten, then eight in place of nine, and so on down until there are no bottles left intact. The children might first hear a recording of the song, or the teacher might sing the first verse to them.

The children learn the tune and the basic lines of the short rhyme, which the teacher will have written on the board. They sing the first verse together. Then eventually the whole group might sing the entire song, or – a more challenging task – the teacher could ask different groups to sing different verses at the appropriate times. The children might also 'dance' the little drama described in the song, and simple 'musical instruments' might be introduced, that some of the children 'play' to accompany the singing and dancing.

The children might then have to copy the first line of the verse from the blackboard into their workbooks, embellishing their writing with colourful borders if they wished. A short number lesson could follow, with the children writing out the numbers 0 to 10, in words and in numerals, or counting up from ten rather than down. The class might be invited to draw bottles, using their creative skills, perhaps painting their drawings later to add to a wall display. And there could be many other integrated activities, all inspired by the theme of the song that they started out learning.

While all of this activity is going on, the teacher encourages, praises and where necessary disciplines the group or individual pupils within it, all the while taking mental notes of their behaviour and performances. What would the teacher be looking out for? Certainly for evidence of 'academic' learning, in this case, of number recognition and counting in numeracy, and communication, understanding, letter recognition and handwriting in literacy. But also for evidence of creative development, in this case music making and creative movement, and aspects of personal, social and emotional development, for example self-confidence, cooperation skills and 'sense of community'.

The creative drawings and any other tangible evidence of achievement could eventually be placed by the teacher into the children's individual progress files, for reference later, for example in meetings with parents or carers, or school inspectors. As a personal *aide-mémoire* for use later in the term, the teacher might jot down a few key points about each child to summarise the observations made throughout the activity sequence.

Further up the school, we could take a Year 2 lesson sequence on minibeasts as another example. The principal teaching objectives (in teacher speak!) are for the children to learn:

1   that a variety of small animals live in the local environment
2   that different animals prefer different habitats within that environment
3   that animals can be grouped according to observable physical characteristics.

The pupils look at pictures of minibeasts, perhaps draw one or two themselves, and then, amongst other things, learn about each minibeast's preferred habitat conditions – woodlice living in cool, damp places, such as under rocks and stones, caterpillars on leaves, spiders in dry, airy locations, and so on. This class-based learning is reinforced by an outing into the school grounds or to the local park to collect minibeasts, to confirm variety and habitat preferences (learning objectives 1 and 2), and to observe physical characteristics at first hand (in readiness for learning objective 3). As minibeasts are observed, and in some cases, gathered, they are identified by name. The teacher will seize the opportunity during the outing to warn the children not to attempt to catch a bee, explaining that bees sting when threatened. And the children will also be urged to gather other minibeasts up gently – not to catch a butterfly by a wing and not to pull a worm roughly out of the ground – since all living creatures should be treated with care and respect, and could be harmed or even killed if mishandled.

Back in class the pupils are introduced to the idea that animals in general, including minibeasts, can be grouped according to their similarities and differences. They are in particular taught that a minibeast is an insect if it has six legs, whatever other physical characteristics it might possess. They are then asked to identify which of the minibeasts they collected earlier is an insect and which is not, introducing them to the concept of classification, or reinforcing this concept if it has been taught earlier in a different context. They might do this by physically sorting the minibeasts into two groups, popping them into jam jars, tins, paper cups or whatever. Or they might sort the minibeasts 'virtually', by 'dragging' coloured images of minibeasts into one or other of two labelled 'virtual jars' as they undertake an exciting computer-based version of the same sorting task. Alternatively, they might be given a relevant paper-based task to do, such as that shown in Figure 2.1.

During the lesson sequence the teacher will have asked the pupils many questions, to draw attention to important points, to stimulate thinking about the topic in general, and informally to assess learning: 'How many legs does a spider have?', 'Is a spider an insect?', 'How can we tell if a spider is an insect or not?', and so on. If a child, or the group as a whole, gives a wrong answer to a question then the teacher can gently correct this, explaining why the answer is incorrect, and can perhaps test the child or group again later to see whether the fact has now been learned and the learning retained.

At the end of the lesson sequence the children might be asked to complete a worksheet, or 'test in disguise'. With the results, the teacher could gain a global assessment of the learning,

Which of these minibeasts are insects?

Figure 2.1 An insect identification task

using this to make a decision about whether any of the taught information needed to be revisited, with an individual child, with a group or with the whole class. The completed work-sheet would be a candidate for inclusion in each child's cumulating portfolio of evidence of achievement.

In a Year 3 class pupils might be carrying out a typical in-class survey, of pet owner-ship, or ice cream flavour preferences, or shoe size. As far as the pupils are concerned, the purpose of the pet survey is to find out how many pupils in the class have dogs, cats, rabbits or some other type of pet. But the teacher's purpose in organising the activity would be to give the pupils practice in simple tallying and chart drawing, and indirectly in chart reading, following numeracy lessons on the topic of data handling. Working within their groups the children keep a tally of pet ownership, as each pupil in the class reveals what kind of pet he or she has. The pupils complete a template tally sheet provided by the teacher (Figure 2.2, which probably has a neater, if less charming, look than most of the children's attempts).

Once all the pupils have told the rest of the class about their pets the tallies are counted, and the pupils begin to record their results in a simple bar chart, using a grid provided by the

Pet	Tally	Count
dog	✓ ✓ ✓ ✓ ✓ ✓	
cat	✓ ✓ ✓ ✓ ✓ ✓	
rabbit	✓ ✓ ✓	
hamster	✓	
bird		
fish	✓ ✓	

Figure 2.2 Partially completed tally sheet

teacher (Figure 2.3 shows the kind of chart that every child might produce in an ideal world!). As the children work the teacher moves from group to group, observing activity, and giving help here and there as needed.

When all the work is done the teacher asks the whole class 'How many children have pet dogs?' or, a more difficult question this, 'How many children in the class have pets?', and expects to be given the appropriate numbers. Incorrect responses would provide opportunities for discussion to remedy problems – careless tallying, inaccurate counting, sloppy chart drawing, faulty addition, and so on. This phase of the work, along with the teacher's observations of group activity during the pet survey itself, serves two important purposes.

First, it provides the teacher with informal assessment evidence of learning, for particular children, for groups and for the whole class. Second, it provides instant instructional feedback to the pupils, so that they immediately discover where problems arose, what mistakes they made, and what they should do in the future to get things right. The teacher would probably follow up this informal assessment of tallying and charting skills later with further in-class tasks, and might then evaluate the effectiveness of the children's learning of the target concepts and skills by using a short test of some kind (we discuss test creation in Chapter 4). Task outputs and test results could be added to the pupils' achievement portfolios.

For a final example, let us take writing. Following a lesson on structuring writing through paragraphing, with the learning objective 'use varied structures to shape and organise text coherently', a Year 6 class teacher asks the pupils to write a short account of their visit the previous week to the local supermarket. To remind them of the visit the teacher engages the class in a short discussion, during which they exchange information about what they did, what they saw, what impressed them most, and so on. The teacher then provides the pupils with further support, suggesting some of the features of the supermarket that they might usefully comment on in their account (size of store, number of customers and checkout desks, variety of goods on sale, and so on), along with a relevant vocabulary list. As the children

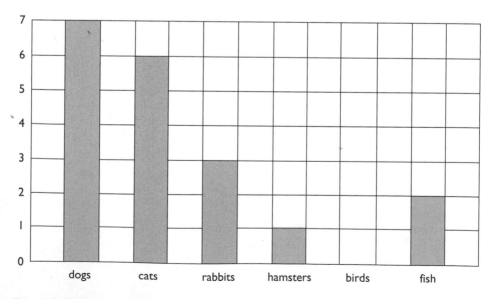

Figure 2.3 Pet survey results bar chart

write the teacher circulates among them, helping occasionally, giving encouragement, and when necessary disciplining to keep the class on task.

When the writing is completed, and before the teacher gathers it in for formal evaluation later, the children are asked to work in pairs to evaluate each other's work. They are reminded about the purpose of paragraphing – to improve readability, control pace and increase impact – and the different ways that paragraphs can be indicated in a text – indenting first sentences, introducing a blank line before each one, using their artistic talents to produce a 'creative' larger first letter, among other strategies. They are asked to keep this information in mind as they judge the positive and negative aspects of each other's writing as regards paragraphing.

The teacher invites feedback from this peer review for the benefit of the whole class, and in this way uses the writing examples to reinforce learning. As the pupils consolidate their learning about paragraph use, the teacher mentally stores evidence of the learning, for the group as a whole and for individual pupils, not just for the new skill of paragraphing, but also for previously taught skills of spelling, punctuation, audience awareness, and so on. This cumulating evidence base for writing skills development will be consolidated when the teacher formally evaluates the new pieces of writing later. Evaluated writing samples could be added into the pupils' portfolios.

With the exception of the reception class, teachers will also from time to time be required to assess their pupils formally, using whatever tests and tasks the school's assessment coordinator will have identified as appropriate, including, where relevant, the external 'government tests' specifically provided for statutory assessment in Year 6. All teachers in every year group will be expected to provide their own judgements about children's current achievement levels in various subject areas. We look at what happens to these assessments in Chapters 6 and 7.

Formative, summative and diagnostic assessment

The examples of teaching, learning and assessment interaction described in the previous section are illustrative of 'formative assessment' activity. But how does 'formative assessment' differ from 'summative assessment', or 'diagnostic assessment'? Are there differences? If so what are they? And what are the similarities? We consider these questions in this section, examining what exactly the different terms imply, always remembering that all assessment is essentially the same process. It is the gathering of evidence about what pupils know, understand, think and can do, and summarising that evidence in some way for evaluation and action of some kind.

Differences between formative assessment and summative assessment simply have to do with frequency, formality, purpose, and the nature and immediacy of consequent action, while diagnostic assessment is concerned with providing evidence of specific strengths and weaknesses in learning, or in ability to learn. The three types of assessment are not necessarily mutually exclusive, as we shall see.

Formative assessment

Observing pupils at work on set tasks, questioning them frequently about their learning, and involving them in discussions about lesson topics, books or their environment, are all activities that class teachers engage in naturally as part of their everyday interaction with pupils in the teaching and learning process. And they are all activities that provide a myriad of assessment opportunities. 'Formative assessment' is the term associated with this kind of ongoing, often almost subconscious, instructionally embedded assessment, examples of which you have come across earlier.

What makes assessment 'formative' is the use the teacher makes of the assessment findings in providing immediate constructive feedback to the pupil. In the words of Black and Wiliam (1998a):

> the term 'assessment' refers to all those activities undertaken by teachers, *and by their students in assessing themselves*, which provide information to be used as feedback to modify the teaching and learning activities in which they are engaged. *Such assessment becomes 'formative assessment' when the evidence is actually used to adapt the teaching work to meet the needs.*
>
> Black and Wiliam 1998a: 2, original italics

Cowie and Bell (1999) defined formative assessment even more succinctly as:

> the process used by teachers and students to recognise and respond to student learning in order to enhance that learning, during the learning.
>
> Cowie and Bell 1999: 3

The Assessment Reform Group (ARG), anxious to clarify formative assessment as 'assessment for learning', described it as:

> the process of seeking and interpreting evidence for use by learners and their teachers, to identify where the learners are in their learning, where they need to go and how best to get there.
>
> ARG 2002a: 1

The term 'formative assessment' derives from the term 'formative evaluation', which was coined in the mid-1960s to distinguish the mid-term evaluation of new educational programmes, at a point where modification would be an option, from the final 'summative evaluation', undertaken when the programme had ended and no further change was possible (Scriven 1967). The programme under evaluation might be a new geography curriculum, a teaching strategy such as synthetic phonics, or the integration of computer-based elements into the existing teaching programme for science.

In the formative evaluation phase a new educational programme is evaluated for strengths and weaknesses, in terms of its associated teaching and learning goals. Should weaknesses be evident, in terms of goals which are not being fully achieved, then if there are relevant ways in which the programme might be modified to address the weaknesses these are identified for implementation. If there is no feasible and affordable remedy then the programme might be discontinued before more time and resource are devoted to it. Alternatively the original programme goals might be modified, to suit what the programme under evaluation was actually capable of achieving. The purpose of formative evaluation is to provide the best chance for a new programme to show its maximum potential, by addressing apparent weaknesses and problems and exploiting strengths before it becomes too late to do so. We look at programme evaluation in Chapter 8.

Formative assessment has similar motivations. But here it is not a question of a one-off mid-term assessment. It is an ongoing cyclic process of assessing, followed immediately by reflection, evaluation and feedback, with, where necessary, action – such as individually helping a child to understand a previously taught concept, or, if the entire class has failed to understand, repeating the lesson or trying an alternative way of explaining the concept.

Another very important difference between formative assessment and formative evaluation is that formative assessment is at least as much about good teaching as it is about assessment *per se*. It is about maximising assessment opportunities for the class teacher, whilst at the same time making teaching and learning potentially more effective by giving pupils regular and constructive assessment feedback, from the teacher, from themselves (self-assessment) and from each other (peer assessment). As Black and Wiliam argue, formative assessment is not only an aspect of teaching, it is 'at the heart of effective teaching' (Black and Wiliam 1998a: 2).

There are many books and research articles available about formative assessment, many of them commissioned or produced by the Assessment Reform Group (ARG). The ARG was originally established in 1990 as the Policy Task Group on Assessment of the British Educational Research Association, partly in reaction to the growing accountability agenda in England and the associated launch of statutory key stage testing, which we will be looking at in detail in Chapter 6. The Group's focus was 'to work on policy issues in relation to assessment and to bring research evidence to the attention of policy makers and practitioners' (ARG 2002a: cover). In particular, the group was concerned with promoting formative assessment practices, also known as 'assessment for learning', in British schools.

The group worked for two decades with the financial support of the Nuffield Foundation, producing several research articles and reports in the process. Among them you will find the seminal article by Black and Wiliam (1998b) that summarises the authors' extensive literature review on formative assessment practice around the world and evidence of its effectiveness in improving learning. The salient findings of the research are highlighted in an associated short document, which reflects on implications for formative assessment in British schools (Black and Wiliam 1998a). Subsequent reports were produced by the ARG (1999, 2002a, 2002b, undated) and Black *et al.* (2002, 2003). Among the many other books that focus exclusively or heavily on formative assessment you will find those of Harlen (2007), Gardner (2006, an ARG publication) and Clarke (2001, 2005, 2008).

If you have read any of these publications, or have participated in initial or CPD courses on formative assessment, then you will be familiar with the principal strategies for teaching and assessing that have been identified as effective. 'Wait time' is one important example. When class teachers pose a question to a group or to the whole class they tend to expect an immediate response from one or other of the pupils, so that they can maintain a relatively fast pace of delivery when contextualising a new lesson or summing up learning. When that instant response does not materialise there is a natural tendency for teachers to provide the answer themselves, or to ask a pupil most likely to be able to answer the question correctly to answer it. The effect of either of these strategies on the majority of the pupils could well be that they become passive listeners, or that they barely listen at all to what the teacher is saying. In consequence, the intended motivational impact of the lesson contextualisation or the reinforcing effect of the learning summary is lost on them.

Equally importantly, providing responses to their own questions, or automatically accepting responses from the most 'dependable' pupils, results in lost opportunities for teachers to supplement assessment evidence for all or most of their pupils. By resisting the temptation to provide an immediate self-response, or to accept an eager contribution from a pupil whose answers are usually correct, teachers give pupils a chance to think about the question, and to formulate answers that otherwise they might not have ventured to offer.

In practice, resisting the temptation means consciously forcing oneself to pause for count-able seconds after posing a question, in the hope that in that time pupils will be able to reflect on the question, gather their thoughts, and offer an answer. Moreover, by deliberately asking one of the quieter or 'less focused' pupils to suggest an answer rather than immediately taking the answer from the 'usual culprits', the most eager ones that are usually right, teachers give other pupils the opportunity to show what they know, and perhaps in the process to become more confident and more engaged, and eventually more successful learners. So that once again an opportunity is created to add assessment evidence for pupils who otherwise might continue to be relatively invisible in assessment terms until formal end-of-year assessment highlights problems that could otherwise have been addressed in good time.

The nature of the questions asked by teachers is also important in stimulating learning and providing assessment possibilities. Short, closed questions of the type 'How many legs do insects have?' would be an efficient way of finding out who in the class had learned the impor-tant fact that insects have six legs. But asking the question in a more open way, for example 'Why is a spider not an insect?', could serve the same purpose, while also inviting pupils to think a little more about the question and about the information they had been intended to learn about how to distinguish insects from other minibeasts. It is generally assumed that the use of direct questions of fact might have a tendency to develop superficial 'rote' learning in pupils, while more open-ended questions could stimulate deeper, more effective, learning. This does not mean that all questioning by teachers should be of the second type and that no recall questions should be asked – a happy balance is all that is needed.

Summative assessment

As its name suggests, summative assessment is essentially assessment that is aimed at 'summing up' the learning achievements of an individual pupil, or indeed of a group, at a particular point in time. The 'summing up' element here is important. For if summative assessment is defined simply as assessment at a particular point in time, then *any* type of assessment would qualify as summative. In that case, when a class teacher asks pupils in the middle of a unit on minibeasts how many legs a spider has this would be considered summa-tive assessment. But this very narrow 'atomistic' assessment would not strictly qualify as summative assessment. So summative assessment is not simply to do with providing a snap-shot of learning at a particular time. The snapshot has to be based on a summary of the outcomes of learning for the individual or group over a given programme of work, which might be a unit, a year-long programme or an entire key stage curriculum.

Neither is the fact that assessment leads to marks or grades a sufficient characteristic for defining 'summative' assessment. Asking children how many legs a spider has will result in right answers from some and wrong answers from others. So the children would by default be classified as those who knew the fact and those who did not, at that point in time. Right and wrong answers could readily be given marks of one and zero, respectively, perhaps to be added to other marks for many other questions at later dates. But even though the assessment is made at a particular point in time *and* results in marks, or classifications (which are usually what grades are all about in external examinations), this is not summative assessment. It remains atomistic assessment, since there is no summarisation of broader learning.

The duration of learning does not have to be long for an assessment to qualify as summa-tive. While a single question about spiders' legs would not qualify as summative assessment, asking a child a whole series of questions about spiders – appearance, life cycle, habitat, food requirements, and so on – would do, since the combination of responses would be evidence of the extent of the child's knowledge and understanding of spiders at the end of the unit. Equally valid as summative assessment would be pupils' responses to a set of questions or tasks that required them to use tables, graphs and charts, reading from one or other or putting information into one or other form. The information used in the questions could come from anywhere in the curriculum, including the unit on minibeasts, in-class surveys, data taken from the local newspaper on milk round sales, or whatever. The outcomes of the assessment would provide information about children's general data handling skills at that particular stage in their learning, and not just about how well they could draw a bar chart to present the results of the in-class pet survey.

As a class teacher you will be able to think of many more examples of assessment of this type that you carry out within your classroom to check on your pupils' learning. When assessment is closely tied to a taught unit, in content and in timing, then it can serve the purposes both of summative and of formative assessment. The results of the assessment tell you about the state of your pupils' learning at that particular time, and because of its direct relevance to material just taught you will be able to use the results in a formative way, i.e. feeding back information to the pupils, giving praise where appropriate, correcting misconceptions, reteaching unlearned facts, and so on. And indeed the results of the 'test-based' assessment will themselves be part of your formative assessment evidence, all of which you will use when you come to 'sum up' each pupil's learning at the end of the school year.

But how confident would you be about pulling together all of the evidence you have recorded throughout the year, on paper, electronically and in your memory, about how each of your individual pupils performed in each unit and across the curriculum, in a way that would produce a fair summative judgement for each of your pupils in each curriculum subject? Is there any chance that you might have been overly generous to one group of pupils over another, to boys in science perhaps, swayed by their greater enthusiasm for certain topics, or to girls in English, because of their greater enjoyment of reading and writing and their general neatness of work? How fairly would you have summed up your evidence of learning achievement for the most disruptive children in your class, or the quietest, or those with special needs? How much credit do you give in your subject assessment for the effort a child might have made to understand in class, even when the learning has proved disappointing?

Research has shown that class teachers can indeed be distracted and unconsciously influenced by these kinds of factors when they assess pupils (Morgan and Watson 2002; Harlen 2004, 2005; Martinez et al. 2009; Burgess and Greaves 2009; Wyatt-Smith and Castleton 2005), leading to unfair assessments for some. While enthusiasm, effort, neatness, personality, and so on, are to some extent inevitable influences on a teacher's perceptions of pupils as individuals and as learners, given the human dynamic that is the primary classroom, they are not legitimate influences on assessment judgements. They create unwanted 'noise' in assessment outcomes, reducing fairness for some pupils.

What can you do to provide the fairest assessments that you can of each of your pupils' learning achievements? You can begin by maintaining your awareness of the fact that children's personal qualities, other than their actual learning achievements, can impact on the evidence of learning that you and other teachers record for them, and on the summing up of that evidence into a final judgement of achievement. Being aware of the issue is half way to avoiding 'bias' in your own assessments.

If a test is to be used to provide a summative assessment after some period of learning, rather than your professional judgement, then the longer the duration of learning the longer the test will have to be to cover the intended content of that learning. The only alternative is to sample the content of the learning so that the testing can be fitted into a manageable package for use in the regular classroom context. Apart from in-class manageability, the test would have to be short enough to avoid consuming too much precious teaching time, as well as to reduce the risk of fatiguing the pupils, and in consequence reducing their chances of showing what they know and can do. But the shorter the test the thinner will be the curriculum sampling involved. Think about all of the work in mathematics that a child would do during the whole of the final four years in the primary school, and then ask yourself what kind of summative assessment could possibly cover all that knowledge – all those abilities and skills – equally well, while satisfying a number of quite important constraints.

No test-based summative assessment spanning four years of learning could meet all of the logistic (and financial) requirements without some loss in terms of assessment quality. If the testing time for each pupil is limited to, say, two hours, how sparse would the unavoidable curriculum sampling be? And what would that say about the value of the test results in terms of providing 'fair' snapshots of the learning achievements of individual pupils? These are questions that we shall consider in some depth in Chapter 5, which focuses on the issue of assessment quality and consequent utility, and again in Chapter 6, where England's current key stage testing regime is reviewed.

Diagnostic assessment

Diagnostic assessment, as its name implies, is essentially focused on identifying strengths and weaknesses. We are all aware of the kinds of clinical diagnostic tests that are carried out in the course of everyday life, whether we have direct experience of such tests or not: blood tests to identify causes of illness, eye tests to expose sight problems that require correction, memory tests to diagnose the onset of dementia, and so on.

In the field of education diagnostic tests have been specially developed to identify physical, physiological and psychological impediments to learning. We can explore reasons for poor performance in class, such as attention deficit disorder, dyslexia, autism, partial sight or hearing problems, if these have not already been diagnosed earlier. Children identified in this way with special learning needs can then be provided with appropriate learning, and assessment, support. This kind of diagnostic assessment is not within the realm of responsibility of class teachers, but as an educational professional you will probably be curious to know how such assessments are carried out, especially if you have children in your class with special educational needs (Spooner 2010).

Putting aside this category of specialised diagnostic tests, we can often use the results of our regular classroom assessments of learning to identify strengths and weaknesses in that learning, for an individual child, for a group or an entire class. Everything you have read earlier about formative assessment practice would suggest to you that a major strength of 'assessment for learning' is its ability to offer diagnostic information about learning. And this is the case. The feedback we give pupils on the basis of our assessments, however we make these, is in essence diagnostic feedback.

Thus, in the minibeasts unit the teacher might have noted that while some children could remember all or most of the facts that they had learned about minibeasts and had grasped the notion of classification by sorting minibeasts into insects and non-insects, others had forgotten most of the facts and could never get the hang of minibeast sorting. Still others would have shown evidence of secure learning of one or other aspect – factual knowledge or classification skill – but not both. The pupils' relative strengths and weaknesses, in these and other areas, would be fed back to them, and those with weaknesses in some respect perhaps brought together in groups for further instruction before facing a new assessment later.

Test-based summative assessment has less potential for offering diagnostic information to pupils or their teachers. But having less potential is not synonymous with having no potential at all. How much potential a general subject test has will depend on the breadth of its curriculum coverage and on its length.

A pair of 45-minute mathematics tests, for example, designed to assess the mathematics curriculum at the end of the primary school will have little potential for diagnostic feedback. In two hours of typical mathematics testing at this level, with each test comprising, say, 20 atomistic questions between them demanding demonstration of a variety of different mathematical skills there are unlikely to be more than four or five questions involving fractions, perhaps two or three on data handling, maybe half a dozen on number skills, and so on. Unless a particular pupil was extremely poor at fractions, four or five questions on this topic would be unlikely to reveal anything robust about the pupil's level of understanding in this area. On the other hand, such a test could reveal strengths and weaknesses for a whole class of pupils, should the weaknesses be general and relatively strong.

Harlen (2006), writing about the relationship between formative and summative assessment, notes similar limitations for special set tasks:

> if the tasks are designed to summarize learning related to general criteria, such as statements of attainment in national curricula, they will not have the detail that enables them to be diagnostic in the degree needed to help specific learning.
>
> Harlen 2006: 108

Because of the numbers of test items that are typically administered in them, large-scale attainment surveys, of the kind discussed in Chapter 7, have a great deal of potential for feeding back diagnostically on pupils' strengths and weaknesses in key curriculum subjects, though this feedback will be at the level of a cohort and will not be available for individual pupils. 'Cognitive diagnostic assessment' is the term newly coined to describe this area of research (Leighton and Gierl 2007), although the type of research involved is not in itself new, as the kind of diagnostic feedback that the Assessment of Performance Unit (APU) surveys in the UK produced in the 1980s would testify: see, for example, Mason and Ruddock (1986) on the progressive understanding of decimals at ages 11 and 15, White (1986) on strengths and weaknesses in writing, and the work of the Children's Learning in Science Project (CLIS) that used APU survey questions to explore misconceptions in science (Brook *et al*. 1984, on 'heat', is an example). Chapter 7 explores the potential of large-scale surveys for this kind of diagnostic feedback.

Record keeping

Assessment record keeping is a great concern for many teachers. How often should you be adding to your assessment records for pupils? How should you record assessment outcomes? How detailed do your records have to be? And so on. With all the advice that is given to you about the value of ongoing formative assessment, and about statutory assessment requirements, it would be understandable if you sometimes felt overwhelmed by the thought of all that assessment, and all that consequent record keeping.

But it should not be such a daunting task. All schools are required by law to develop an assessment and record keeping policy and to enforce this throughout the school. Your school's assessment coordinator will have drafted your school's policy, and will have all the necessary forms available for recording the results of statutory assessments in the right way.

You can expect the same support for any other assessments of your pupils that your school, rather than the government, requires you to make, such as using particular commercial tests at particular times in the year, and/or providing your own summative judgement of each pupil's state of progress in one or more subjects.

For other types of assessment, particularly formative assessment, there will probably be no hard and fast rules. Unless your school's assessment and record keeping policy addresses this issue directly, then you are likely to have total freedom to make as few or as many notes as you care to, as seldom or as frequently as you wish, as briefly or as copiously as suits your style, on paper or electronically. That is, provided only that should you be asked to justify your summative assessments at any point, by your headteacher or perhaps by a parent or inspector, then you will be able to do so by referring to your assessment records, as well as to the evidence of your pupils' achievements that you and they will have been storing in their progress portfolios.

Questions for reflection

- Thinking about your own classroom experience, what proportional mix of factual recall and more open questions would you say you typically use in your teaching? Is the mix relatively constant across the curriculum, or does it vary from subject to subject – for example from mathematics to English to environmental studies? Would you change your questioning approach in any way, and if so how?
- What is your view about the potential for improving learning of 'wait time'? Is the potential equal for all pupil groups, do you think? Can you explain your thinking?
- Have you ever used test results in a formative way? If so, can you think back to an occasion when you did this, and evaluate how successfully you managed to get useful formative feedback for your pupils out of the test results?
- Would you judge your record keeping of children's learning progress to be appropriate and manageable? Is there room for improvement? If so, can you suggest some improvement possibilities?

Further reading

Clarke, S. (2008) *Active Learning through Formative Assessment*, London: Hodder and Stoughton.

Gardner, J., Harlen, W., Hayward, L. and Stobart, G. with Montgomery, M. (2010) *Developing Teacher Assessment,* Maidenhead: Open University Press.

Harlen, W. (2007) *Assessment of Learning,* London: Sage.

Swaffield, S. (ed.) (2008) *Unlocking Assessment*, Oxford: Routledge.

Chapter 3

The building blocks of assessment

What are the different ways in which we can assess pupils in the primary classroom? What kinds of questions can we put to them, and in what form? If we give them tasks and activities to do, what might these look like? What would we actually be looking for in the pupils' responses and performances that we would consider as relevant evidence of learning? These questions underpin Chapter 3, which considers the following topics:

- constructed response and select response items
- matching, sequencing and labelling items
- performance assessment tasks
- writing assessment tasks.

Test items and tasks

As we have seen in Chapter 2, assessing pupils in the classroom typically involves asking them questions about what they have learned or about what they think about various matters, or setting them tasks to do that demand the application of 'target' knowledge and skills, observing them at work, and perhaps rating the outcome. In other words the principal methods we use in the classroom to assess pupil learning, and which we use in assessment more generally, are:

- questioning
- observing
- evaluating products.

Questions are sometimes necessarily oral, as in the assessment of mental mathematics or of word pronunciation. Or they are 'written', as in the 'pencil and paper' assessment of reading, or the ICT-based assessment of geographical knowledge.

Observation can happen in real time, for example as pupils discuss a given stimulus in their English lesson, such as 'endangered species', 'global warming' or 'suitable prizes for sports day', or as they carry out an investigation in science, act out a short scene in drama, or measure lengths and weights in mathematics. Or it could take place after the event, for example when video recordings of pupils undertaking practical tasks or engaging in role play are later viewed and pupil performances assessed.

Product evaluation typically takes place after the event, although in the classroom there could be ongoing assessment as the product develops. The product might be a poster, or a three-dimensional model, or a wall display, or a concept map, or a portfolio of work, or a piece of fictional writing, among many other possibilities.

How we assess depends on what we set out to assess, i.e. what our assessment objectives are. But before we move on to consider assessment objectives and the degree to which these determine the most appropriate assessment strategy, let us first overview some of the variety of types of question that we can use in pupil assessment, and with which we create tests. A 'question' in this context can literally be a single short question, such as 'What is 20 multiplied by 15?', or it can be an instruction 'Mark the place on the map where the new school is to be located', or it might be a combination of a question and a request, such as 'What did the Romans use to make foundations for their roads?' followed by 'Explain why they made foundations that way …'. The question becomes a 'test item' only when some assessment criteria are attached to it, in the form of a mark scheme.

Among the large variety of test items that are used in assessment are two principal types: 'select' items, sometimes known as 'objective' items, and 'supply', or 'constructed response', items. The essential difference between the two is that in the first type the answer to the question is actually presented to the pupil, among a set of answer options that includes incorrect answers (the most common item formats are 'multiple-choice' and 'multiple-response'), while in the second type the answer must be 'constructed' unaided by the pupil (principal formats are 'short-answer', 'open-ended' and 'extended response'). The first type of question is considered to tap 'passive' knowledge with the second type tapping 'active' knowledge (for a useful guide on item types and their development see, for example, SQA 2009). We begin by looking at some examples of constructed response items.

Constructed response formats

Constructed response items come in two principal forms: 'short-answer' and 'open-ended' (sometimes known as 'extended response', depending on the volume of written response required).

Short-answer items

In short-answer forms the pupil typically responds to the question by supplying single words or short phrases, or numbers. For example:

- 'What is the capital city of France?'
- 'Who led the first Roman invasion of Britain?'
- 'How many legs do insects have?'
- 'Calculate 50×5'
- 'What is happening to your ice cream when it starts running down the cone?'
- 'Heidi had 10 sweets that she shared with four friends. How many sweets did Heidi and each of her friends have?'.

Such questions might be asked orally, in which case the numeracy questions just described would be assessing mental mathematics, or they might be presented on paper or on screen. Figure 3.1 shows the 'Paris' example as it might appear in print, while a second short-answer example, from mathematics, is given in Figure 3.2.

Other examples used frequently in reading comprehension tests include summary completion and sentence completion, both of which require pupils to use syntactically

What is the capital city of France?

Answer _____

Figure 3.1 A short-answer question

It is Christmas and the class is decorating a tree with stars.
There are 22 children and each child has 7 stars.

How many stars are there altogether?

Answer _____ stars

Figure 3.2 Short-answer question (adapted from SSA 2006: figure C4a)

and semantically appropriate words to fill gaps left by prior word deletions. The items in Figure 3.3 are examples of sentence completion, while the multi-item task in Figure 3.4 is a summary completion exercise. Both examples are based on a story of a little boy, Jason, who becomes marooned on an island when his rowing boat drifts away from the shore (text not shown). Usually an exact response to every 'gap item' is to be found in the source text, so that to a greater or lesser extent such items assess simple information retrieval, although there is scope for pupils to use alternative equally appropriate words (such as 'worried' in place of the 'anxious' in the text).

Complete the following sentences by putting a word in each gap

1   As the boat drifted further and further from the shore
     Jason began to feel _____ .

2   Jason's little dog barked loudly when she saw the _____
     loom out of the mist.

Figure 3.3 Sentence completion items

Here is a summary of the story after the wind had started to rise. Fill each gap with one or more words. Use words from the story or your own words.

Jason was _____ being in the boat so much that he

eventually _____ asleep. He woke to find that the

_____ was beginning to _____ and mist

was _____ to surround them. As the boat drifted

_____ and further from _____ Jason began to

feel _____ . His little dog barked _____ when

she saw the _____ loom out of the mist.

Figure 3.4 A typical summary completion task in reading

Note that several different test items could be produced from one single sentence, simply by deleting different constituent words. Thus, in the first sentence in Figure 3.3, the deleted word could have been 'boat', or 'drifted', or one of the instances of 'further', or 'from', or 'the', and so on.

Different word deletion choices are equally possible in the summary completion task in Figure 3.4. The specific assessment purpose of the task, and its associated mark scheme, should justify the deletions actually made and the nature of the response that would be considered acceptable. Both summary completion and sentence completion derive from the cloze procedure, which was introduced over 50 years ago to assess the readability of texts (Taylor 1953). In summaries, word deletions can be systematically random, in the sense that every nth word is deleted. Or word deletions can be specifically selected to focus on 'meaning-carrying' words, which is a common strategy when summary completion exercises are used to assess reading comprehension. Alternatively, deletions can be specifically chosen to contribute to the assessment of some aspect of knowledge of language, in which case verb forms, say, could be deletion targets. For this purpose the task could be presented 'cold', that is without a source text.

When presented cold, the range of word choices in sentence completion items and summary completion tasks can be greater than in a source-based situation, because there is no longer a need to faithfully reflect the information presented in the source text. Look, for instance at the second and last sentences in the summary in Figure 3.4. There are several possible syntactically and semantically appropriate word insertions that could be chosen by a pupil to complete these sentences. But they would not all be relevant in terms of the story line in the passage the pupil had previously read. In the second sentence, for example, 'the *wind* was beginning to *rise*' would follow the story line, whereas 'the *boat* was beginning to *sink*' or 'the *siren* was beginning to *sound*' would not.

Sentence completion items and summary completion tasks can be accompanied by a set of words from among which the pupil could choose a suitable one to insert into each gap. In this case the item/task would no longer be a constructed response item/task. Sentence completion items would become multiple-choice items (see the section on 'Selected response formats'), while a scaffolded summary completion task ('aided summary completion') would become a 'matching' task (see the section on 'Matching, sequencing and labelling').

As an alternative to words, short phrases or numbers as responses to short-answer items, pupils can instead be invited to take an action of some kind. This could be plotting coordinates, drawing lines of symmetry, adding bars to a bar chart to reflect given information, drawing lines on an image of a clock face to show a given time (or setting a clock to a given time if the task was carried out practically), shading blocks in a grid to indicate a fractional area, and so on.

The second item in Figure 3.5 is an 'action' example for very young children that in principle taps the same piece of knowledge as the more traditional short-answer item shown in the same figure. An important difference between these two items is the time that a child might take to respond. While probably not an issue in regular class time, such items could pose important problems if used in time-constrained written tests. How often have you found a child taking for ever just to write 'today's date' at the top of a worksheet?

Chart construction items are similarly vulnerable, some pupils taking so long over their chart creation that they would risk being 'timed out' before finishing the test. This is why chart completion items are more often used in numeracy tests to tap data representation skills. The bar chart shown in Figure 2.3 (Chapter 2), in which there is no bar showing against 'birds', could be transformed into a chart completion item (Figure 3.6), with pupils required to transfer given data into the chart by drawing the missing bar.

Extended response questions

Essays and reports are clear examples of extended response questions. But between these and short-answer questions are many possibilities, and there really is no precise point at which a short-answer question becomes an open-ended or extended response question. It is a matter of judgement, and depends not only on the intention of the item writer but also on the response of the pupil being assessed. Item writers might develop questions that are designed to elicit a paragraph or more of response text, but it is the pupil respondents who actually decide how much text is in practice produced, and it is not necessarily the case that the more text that is produced the higher the marks achieved!

Imagine, for example, the variety of responses that pupils might offer in response to the question 'Why did Jason feel so afraid as darkness began to fall?'. One pupil might provide a fairly full and accurate response, such as 'Jason felt afraid because when he woke up he saw that his boat was drifting in the wind, and he couldn't see the shore any more because of the dark. So he didn't know what to do, and that made him afraid', another might say 'Because

How many legs does a spider have?	This is a drawing of a spider. But it has no legs yet. Can you draw the spider's legs?
Answer _____	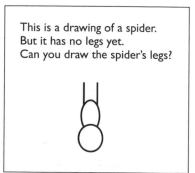

Figure 3.5 Constructed response items

This chart shows how many pupils in a class had different kinds of pet.
Add a bar to show that 5 pupils had birds.

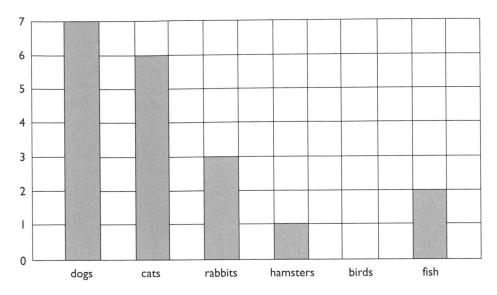

Figure 3.6 A chart completion item

he couldn't see the shore any more', a third might simply offer 'He was afraid of the dark', while quite a few others would probably not make an attempt to respond at all.

Extended response questions are commonly used in a variety of subjects: Figure 3.7 shows another example, this time from geography. Once again you might try imagining the kinds of responses that Year 6 pupils might offer.

> The River Rhine is in danger! It is heavily affected by pollution of different kinds. Explain how one source of pollution, untreated sewage, damages the river.

Figure 3.7 A geography 'extended response' question

Non-response is a problem with open-ended questions in general, and in pencil-and-paper tests the more 'extended' the expected response the higher the non-response rate tends to be:

> there was a very strong association between format and success rates, with open formats producing lower attainment on average than closed format, partly because of the impact of substantially higher non-response rates.
>
> AAP 2005a: 15

Selected response formats

Multiple-choice items

Figures 3.8 and 3.9 are examples of 'multiple-choice' items, probably the most commonly used 'select' format. Here, pupils are asked a question, or given an instruction, and are presented with several response options to choose among. The question or instruction to which pupils must respond is technically termed the 'stem' – in the first item this is 'How many legs does a spider have?' and in the second 'Tick (✓) the symmetric pattern'. The correct answer is the 'key', and the wrong answers presented among the response options are 'distractors'. In principle the item in Figure 3.8 taps exactly the same piece of scientific knowledge as the items shown earlier in Figure 3.5, but 'passively'.

Multiple-choice is considered to be an efficient item format, particularly for assessing factual recall, but also for assessing conceptual understanding – though items are often more difficult to construct for this purpose. The number of answer options in such items is most typically four or five, but the number can be higher or lower.

The lower the number of options the higher the chance that a pupil could arrive at the right answer through guessing. A special case of a multiple-choice item, with just two answer options and with therefore a 50–50 chance of choosing the right answer, is the familiar 'true–false' item (in various guises). An example would be an item that presents just one, any one, of the patterns shown in Figure 3.9 with a question like 'Is this pattern symmetrical? Yes or No' or 'Sophie says this is a symmetrical pattern. Is she right or wrong?'.

Because of the high probability of achieving a correct answer in a non-valid way such items are not good forms of assessment. They are best used as a non-credit lead-in to a follow-on question, such as 'Why do you say that?' or 'Why do you think so?', that would anticipate an open-ended response showing evidence (or not) of understanding of some underlying piece of subject knowledge or concept.

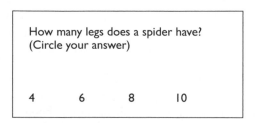

Figure 3.8 An example multiple-choice question

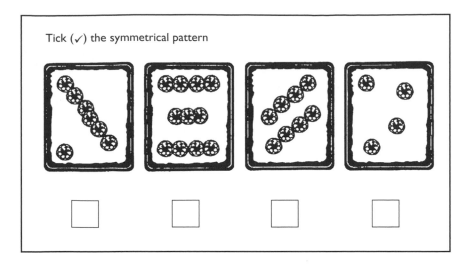

Figure 3.9 An example multiple-choice mathematics question (Source: AAP 2005b: 8)

Multiple-response items

'Multiple-response' items are similar to multiple-choice items. The difference is that in multiple-response items there is more than one correct response option among any number of alternative response options, and all of the correct options must be selected for the response to be considered correct. We have seen an example of such an item in Figure 2.1 (Chapter 2), in which pupils are to select which of six minibeasts are insects. Pupils might be offered a degree of help when answering such items, in the form of an indication about how many of the options they would need to choose as meeting the given criterion, such as 'Which *two* of these minibeasts are insects?'. Or, as in Figure 2.1, they might be offered no help at all in this regard. The item in Figure 3.10 is another example that offers no help to pupils.

The different possible combinations of number of response options, number of correct response options, and degree of scaffolding offered, can pose issues for deciding appropriate mark allocations (technically known as mark 'tariffs') and for performance interpretation.

Matching, sequencing and labelling

There are a number of item formats that are neither 'select' nor 'supply' in any pure sense. One of these is 'matching', in which the pupil is essentially required to match elements in one list with those in another. The lists might be body organs to be matched with physiological functions (stomach with digestion, heart with circulation, …) , materials to be matched against properties or uses, capital cities to be matched with countries, minibeasts to be matched with habitats, and so on.

In the item in Figure 3.11 one list comprises pictures of electrical circuit components while the other is composed of conventional circuit symbols. Circuit components are to be matched with their conventional symbols. Note that while there are three pictures of components in this item there are four circuit symbols. It is not necessary for the two lists to have the same number of members, and there are no rules about how unequal they might be.

Which of the following things happened as Jason's boat was drifting out to sea?

a)   the mist came down ☐

b)   his little dog barked ☐

c)   his boat capsized ☐

d)   the wind rose ☐

e)   he used his mobile to call for help ☐

Figure 3.10 An example multiple-response question

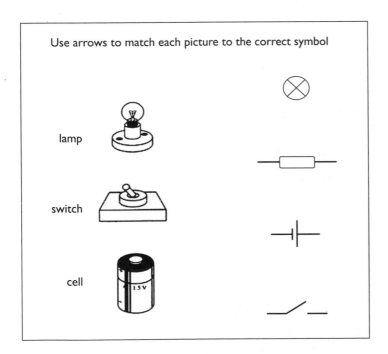

Use arrows to match each picture to the correct symbol

lamp

switch

cell

Figure 3.11 An example matching item in science (Source: item adapted from AAP 2005a: 12)

A related format is 'sequencing'. The essential difference between sequencing and matching is that the matching involved in sequencing is temporal. In this type of item pupils are required to take an unordered set of pictures or symbols, words or phrases, and to use the elements of that set to create a sequentially ordered list. A popular example frequently used in reading comprehension tests is a randomly ordered set of sentences that the pupil has to reorder to reflect the correct sequence in a story line. Figure 3.12 is an example that once again relates to the story of Jason and his rowing boat. In science assessment, frequently used sequencing items are those in which missing elements, usually animal names or images, must be inserted into a food chain, or the appropriate elements slotted into a life-cycle diagram.

Another related item format is 'labelling', in which the pupil has to match words in a list with indicated parts in a diagram of a plant, human body, geological cross-section, or whatever. In Figure 3.13 there are just as many plant part names presented to the respondent as there are labels to be added to the drawing, but the number of part names could have been larger.

These item types differ from the 'select' and 'supply' types in one particularly important way, and this is the strong dependence among pupils' response decisions. Once a list or set member has been used in a matching, sequencing or labelling item it usually should not be reused. This therefore reduces the options available for a second, then third, then fourth match. Unless one of the lists is longer than the other then eventually the final match is a default match. It would therefore make little sense to think about awarding part marks for correct matches, correct sequence locations, or correct labelling. The whole item must be answered correctly for the pupil to be deemed to have shown evidence of the skill, knowledge or concept being assessed, and only then would the total mark be merited. But maybe you disagree?

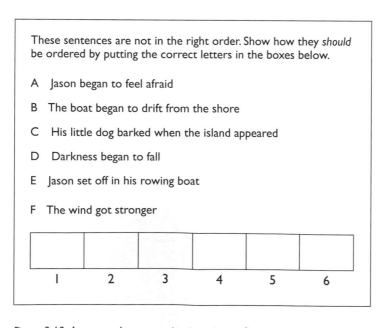

These sentences are not in the right order. Show how they *should* be ordered by putting the correct letters in the boxes below.

A   Jason began to feel afraid

B   The boat began to drift from the shore

C   His little dog barked when the island appeared

D   Darkness began to fall

E   Jason set off in his rowing boat

F   The wind got stronger

1	2	3	4	5	6

Figure 3.12 An example sequencing item in reading

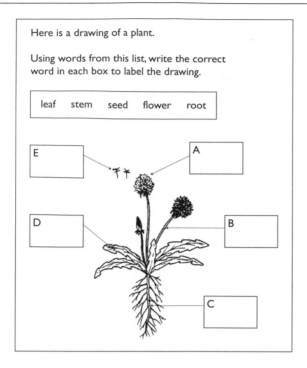

Here is a drawing of a plant.

Using words from this list, write the correct word in each box to label the drawing.

| leaf   stem   seed   flower   root |

E

A

D

B

C

Figure 3.13 An example labelling item in science

One important difference between the labelling item and the regular type of matching item is that if the plant part names were taken away then the item would become a constructed response item, or rather a collection of independent 'supply' items. At this point marks could justifiably be given for every plant part correctly labelled. The only reason for requesting that more than one part be labelled would be to exploit testing time and space by maximising use of the same resource (the plant diagram).

Multi-item tasks

The different item formats just described can also be combined into 'multi-part questions', also known as 'structured questions' or 'multi-item tasks'. The labelling item shown in Figure 3.13, if converted into a constructed response format, would technically be a multi-item task, every plant part to be labelled becoming a separate item that could have been presented alone, and each having its own mark allocation. The summary completion exercise shown in Figure 3.4 is also essentially a multi-item task, though in this case there is a degree of dependence among the items, and not every sentence completion item within the whole summary could realistically be presented alone. In both these examples the constituent items share the same format. But this need not be the case. Any combination of formats is permissible within a composite task.

Figure 3.14 is just one example. The first item in this composite task is the question 'Where do you think he found the woodlice?'. The second is the unwritten question 'Why do you think that's where he found the woodlice?'. The first item is a conventional multiple-choice (or multiple-response?) item, with four answer options. The second question is asking for an open-ended extended response, showing evidence of knowledge that woodlice prefer to live in cool, damp places. Both question parts might be awarded marks, or marks might be allocated only to the second part.

Performance assessment tasks

'Performance assessment' is a term coined in the late 1980s to describe the assessment of individuals' abilities to draw on a variety of relevant knowledge and skill in order to perform an authentic 'holistic' task in a practical context. The tasks used in performance assessment tend by their nature to be relatively long, certainly when compared with the 'atomistic' items and tasks that are typically used in paper-based and screen-based tests, such as those shown

Figure 3.14 A science test question demanding two responses (Source: item adapted from APU 1979: 10)

in Figures 3.1 to 3.14. They are often also, by their nature, administered to pupils individually, although individual assessment within a group task is also quite common.

In a practically-based music assessment, for example, a pupil might, among other tasks, be required to play one or two pieces, one practised and one unseen, and on this basis would be assessed for technical skills, sight reading skills and 'musicality'. The assessment of drama, dance and other performance arts also by its nature involves some element of performance assessment, as does the assessment of collaboration skills, discussion skills, oral presentation skills, and so on. Pupils' science investigation skills, mathematics application skills, and speaking and listening skills are all assessed through active demonstration, i.e. through performance assessment.

Practical performances of these broader kinds are not as readily 'marked' as are atomistic items. They are usually rated by an observer – the pupil's class teacher in most cases – who judges the quality of the performance, aspect by aspect and/or holistically, generally with reference to some given text-based criteria contained in a 'rubric' (i.e. a rating scheme), or in a set of performance descriptors, such as the level descriptions in the English National Curriculum (see Appendix 2).

Numerous, often very imaginative, performance tasks have been developed by various individuals and organisations. A handful of examples will provide a flavour of the kinds of activity that performance tasks can demand of pupils. As a first example we can consider a task that was designed to assess pupils' speaking (and listening) skills. The task happens once again to focus on the humble spider! Two pupils (11-year-olds) first listen to an audio recording of how spiders build their webs, and show their understanding of the recording by arranging six drawings into the correct sequence to represent the different stages in the web building process (Figure 3.15 – a sequencing item).

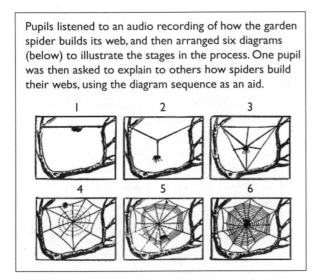

Figure 3.15 A speaking and listening performance task (Source: MacLure and Hargreaves 1986: 27)

One of the pupils then uses the drawings as an aid as he or she describes the web building process to another pair of pupils who have not heard the audio recording or seen the pictures. An observer rates the pupil's communication skills for 'assimilation of information about a process, acquired through listening' and 'conveying the information clearly to listeners', with a later independent rating based on an audio recording of the task performance (MacLure and Hargreaves 1986: 27; for full details see Gorman *et al.* 1984: chapter 2).

Another speaking task that involved a pair of pupils interacting focused on 'describing and persuading'. The pupils were first asked by an assessor to identify and describe their favourite games, giving their reasons for liking that game. They were then asked to imagine that they had time to play just one of the games, and to argue for their own game in an attempt to persuade the other pupil to choose that game to play. The pupils, whose performances were audio recorded, were rated immediately by impression, for describing and for persuading separately, using a 1–7 rating scale, and were rated again later, for linguistic expression, on the basis of the recording (for details see Price *et al.* 1986).

Other task possibilities include having pupils, working individually with an administrator (often their class teacher) or in pairs:

- describe what they see in a picture or in a set of pictures
- use a set of pictures as a prompt for story telling
- explain why a particular job interests them
- listen to a recorded anecdote before recounting a personal experience of their own
- talk about their favourite book or film.

What is important in any assessment of speaking and listening is that the pupils being assessed cooperate fully with the assessor in showing evidence of their oracy skills. For a task to 'work' well, i.e. to stimulate pupil reaction and willingness to talk, it should be interesting and enjoyable for pupils to undertake, and it should have a clear purpose and outcome.

Small-group discussions are another popular way to observe pupils interacting with one another. Discussions not only provide opportunities to assess pupils' speaking and listening skills, but also their collaboration and problem solving skills. Again, the topic of discussion needs to be such as to interest and motivate pupils, so that they do interact with each other, listening to others' contributions and hopefully making contributions of their own in a constructive way. But there is an important question mark over the assessment of individual pupils as they work within groups. This is the extent to which a particular pupil's performance in the group might be supported or hindered by the personalities and capabilities of other group members. In other words, there are questions about the validity and the reliability of pupil assessment in group tasks.

Like speaking and listening, the authentic assessment of science investigation skills similarly demands that pupils be assessed as they demonstrate their skills practically. The Assessment of Performance Unit (APU) science survey programme (briefly described in Chapter 7) was a pioneer in this area – see Harlen (1988) for an overview of APU performance assessment experience. Many different investigation tasks have been conceived to motivate and challenge pupils, with 'research questions' like the following (Harlen 1984; Welford *et al.* 1985; AAP 2005a):

- 'Which kind of paper will hold the most water?'
- 'Which food do mealworms prefer?'
- 'How can you speed up rate of dissolving?'

- 'What combination of conditions do woodlice prefer: damp and dark, dry and dark, damp and light, dry and light?'
- 'Does everything stick to a magnet in the same way?'
- 'Do different materials have different insulation properties?'
- 'How do different materials respond to being squashed?'

The pupil is typically asked the research question, and presented with a set of relevant resources, not all of which need be necessary for investigating the question. The pupil is then observed and rated for different aspects of performance as the investigation progresses, typically using a checklist. You might not be surprised to hear that boys have been found to be generally more enthusiastic than girls about engaging in this kind of investigative activity: 'differences between boys and girls ... indicate a consistently greater enthusiasm for involvement of the boys' (Harlen 1984: 158).

Writing assessment tasks

In order to assess a pupil's writing skills in any meaningful way the pupil really does need to be required to produce a piece of writing, and preferably more than one piece, of some pre-specified kind. Since writing involves the coordinated application of various pieces of knowledge about language, including the 'technical' skills of spelling and grammar, along with learned concepts about style appropriateness, text structure, and so on, writing assessment has much in common with performance assessment as described above. The difference is that we do not usually rate pupils' writing skills as they 'perform' the act of writing. Writing ability is typically assessed by rating the product of the writing, i.e. the piece of writing actually produced, in the same way that creative and functional skills, such as sculpture, painting, woodworking, and so on, are assessed through product evaluation.

Many different writing purposes can provide a stimulus for writing, including story telling, reporting, summarising, persuading, instructing, among others. And the form of writing varies to suit the writing purpose: narrative prose, numbered paragraphs, telegraphic writing, bullet points, etc. For example, pupils might be asked to write:

- a letter to the local council to protest about the closure of a local post office
- a short story about an alien who falls down a chimney
- a report about a little dog found abandoned in the school car park
- a summary of how the Romans built their roads.

Which of the various possibilities a teacher, or some other assessor, chooses to use in assessment will depend on the specific objectives of the assessment, and in particular on the chosen definition of the meaning of 'writing ability' for the age group of pupils being assessed.

One of the biggest problems faced in the formal assessment of writing is ensuring that the pupil is sufficiently motivated by the given writing task, a) to write something, b) to produce enough writing for rating to be meaningful or even simply feasible, and c) to write as well as possible so that the assessment will be a fair reflection of the pupil's genuine capabilities. In normal classroom situations it will not be difficult for class teachers to get most pupils writing. The writing is usually preceded by one or more other activities, such as reading or discussing, that serve to introduce the topic and purpose of the writing. But in an external formal summative assessment context there is often little, if any, time for pre-writing orientation, the pupil having essentially to write 'cold'. We consider this issue further in Chapter 5.

Questions for reflection

- What would you see as the advantages and the disadvantages of 'supply' versus 'select' items in assessment? Is one item type more or less appropriate than the other in different subjects? How often do you use each item type in your own in-class assessment, oral or written?
- Good quality multiple-choice items can be quite difficult to produce. Can you think why?
- Group discussions and practical investigations in science are common activities in today's primary classroom. But they are time consuming, and while they have value in teaching they can be tricky to use for assessment. Why should this be?
- Have you ever faced serious challenges in trying to motivate your pupils to produce more than a sentence of prose in a writing activity? If so, how did you solve the problem, if you did solve it? And what tips would you give other teachers about the kinds of writing task that work well with pupils of different ages?

Further reading:

AAP (2005a) *Sixth Survey of Science 2003*, an Assessment of Achievement Programme report, Edinburgh: Scottish Executive Education Department. Available online at http://www.scotland.gov.uk/Publications/2005/03/20882/54916, accessed 25 May 2011.

AAP (2005b) *Seventh Survey of Mathematics 2004*, an Assessment of Achievement Programme report, Edinburgh: Scottish Executive Education Department. Available online at http://www.scotland.gov.uk/Publications/2005/10/2192247/22481, accessed 25 May 2011.

Anderson, P. and Morgan, G. (2008) *Developing Tests and Questionnaires for a National Assessment of Educational Achievement*. Washington: The World Bank.

SQA (2009) *Guide to Assessment*, Glasgow: Scottish Qualifications Authority. Available online at http://www.sqa.org.uk/sqa/files_ccc/GuideToAssessment.pdf, accessed 25 May 2011.

Chapter 4

Creating, using and interpreting tests

When we assess 'learning' what exactly do we think that we are assessing? How can we choose among all the different types of assessment item and task that are available to ensure that they, and any tests that they might become part of, are appropriate, in the sense of being 'fit for purpose'? How would you assess learning in each of several different curriculum areas through formal testing of relatively short duration? Chapter 4 considers these and related questions. It discusses:

* Assessment aims and objectives
* Test types and marking
* Creating tests
* Interpreting test scores
* Norm-referenced and criterion-referenced assessment.

Assessment aims and objectives

In the previous chapter we saw many of the possible item and task types available for use in assessment. But how should you choose among them to ensure that they, and any tests that they might become part of, are appropriate, in the sense of being 'fit for purpose'? Would a test containing only multiple-choice items be the most appropriate? Such a test would certainly be quick to mark. Or should it be a test made up of a mixture of select and supply items? Should multi-item tasks feature, to give pupils a small degree of contextualisation? Would a pencil-and-paper test be the right choice, or should the test be a practical one? The answer to all these questions is that your assessment objectives should guide both your test creation and your item selection choices.

Every process of assessment should have clear aims and objectives. These will specify what is intended to be assessed, to enable us to draw out the right kind of evidence of learning and achievement with the most appropriate assessment tools. In particular, you, as classroom teacher, will want to be sure when assessing pupils, however informally, that the responses and behaviours elicited from them are relevant in terms of the learning objectives that you and your class have been working towards.

Suppose that you are working with your class of Year 2 pupils through the minibeast lesson sequence described in Chapter 2. You should all the time be linking activity to the underlying teaching objectives. In your assessments of the pupils throughout the lesson sequence and later, you should be focusing on these particular teaching objectives, which are readily transformed into assessment objectives (Table 4.1).

Table 4.1 Teaching and assessment objectives for the minibeast lesson sequence

Teaching–learning objectives	Assessment objectives
Pupils to learn: • that a variety of small animals live in the local environment, called minibeasts • the names and physical characteristics of local minibeasts • that different animals prefer different habitats • that animals can be grouped according to observable physical characteristics.	Assess whether the pupil can: • name at least ten of the minibeasts that can be found locally • identify particular minibeasts by their appearance • identify which habitats particular minibeasts prefer • distinguish insects from other minibeasts by the fact that they have six legs.

It is assessment objectives that should determine what questions teachers ask their pupils, what tasks they give them to do and what observations they make of them as they work. In our constrained example, where the objectives are few in number and relatively easily interpreted, it is not difficult to imagine the kinds of questions and activities that you could use in assessment. For example, the children could be shown a selection of minibeasts and asked to write down their names in a worksheet (essentially constructed response items). Or they could be given a sheet of paper with pictures of minibeasts and a collection of minibeast names, and asked to match names to pictures (a matching item). Other oral questions or worksheet items could be used to explore knowledge of habitats, and we have seen from Chapters 2 and 3 other relevant possibilities for tapping factual and conceptual knowledge.

However the assessment takes place, whenever it takes place, and whatever strategies you might use to explore the pupils' learning, the principal objectives of the assessment must be at the forefront. Whatever other information you impart to pupils during the minibeast lessons, whatever other topics you might have covered in discussion with them, it is the particular pieces of knowledge about minibeasts that you should aim to focus on in assessment, and nothing else.

The assessment should not be influenced by how tidily a pupil can draw a spider or a snail, or how well-behaved the pupil was during the out-of-class minibeast search, or how enthusiastic a pupil might have been about sorting the minibeasts into jam jars to separate the insects from the rest. What you need to concentrate on gathering evidence about should be the number of relevant minibeasts that the pupil can correctly name, whether the pupil can correctly match minibeasts to habitat preferences, and whether the 'six legs' criterion for identifying insects has been learned. The results of the assessment can then be used forma-tively or summatively, depending on when and how the assessment takes place and what its principal purpose is.

This is not to say that teachers should try always to avoid assessing other attributes as they teach pupils about a particular topic. Indeed, teachers use, and should use, every possible opportunity to gather evidence with which to assess various pupil characteristics, such as enthusiasm for learning, collaboration skills, self-esteem, creative skills, and so on. But evidence of this kind should be kept separate from the evidence gathered about the specific 'academic' learning that is our central concern here.

Wherever possible, assessment objectives should closely match learning objectives, as they do in the case of the minibeast lesson sequence. But there are many occasions when it is not possible to achieve such a close correspondence in the context of formal assessment. One reason is that formal tests usually have to sample the 'domain of learning', the 'programme of study', that has been the subject of teaching and learning over some period of time. A curriculum typically comprises long lists of pieces of information that children must learn, and of skills that children are expected to acquire. There might be a hundred or more of them. Every one of the elements in the list will give rise to a teaching objective, a learning intention, in lesson planning. But not every detailed teaching objective can possibly be assessed in the relatively short time span that formal tests are typically allowed.

How would you set out to test how much learning a pupil had gained by the end of primary school in each subject area in the curriculum, given the amount of subject matter and the wide range of skills and abilities that will have been covered in the classroom in each case? Think, for instance, about a pupil's:

* reading ability
* writing skills
* historical knowledge
* mathematical ability
* science knowledge and understanding
* creative skills
* listening skills.

More importantly, how would you assess learning in each of these areas through formal testing of relatively short duration?

Clearly, you could only hope to sample the curriculum in each case. Take a 45-minute test at age 11 intended broadly 'to assess pupils' numeracy skills' with reference to a four-year programme of study. There will be room in the test for only a handful of items to represent each of the major skills – among which will be the four number skills, handling fractions, and reading from tables and charts. In heavily content-based subjects like science and history the sampling will in some sense be even more severe, with whole chunks of the knowledge curriculum necessarily excluded from the test.

In addition to the constraints imposed by the inevitable need to sample the curriculum, other circumstances can also sometimes lead to a reduction in curriculum representation. We might all agree that science investigation skills should feature in any formal assessment of science in the primary school, and that the investigations should span the science content curriculum. But in practice it is difficult to organise robust formal assessment of investigation skills with individual children, given their time-consuming nature. It is particularly difficult to include investigations featuring 'life processes and living things' for this reason: think of an investigation to explore the effect of light and humidity on the rate of germination and growth of daffodil bulbs, or an investigation to establish the habitat preferences of wood-lice, snails and spiders. Moreover, where living things are concerned, however small and commonplace they might be, there are issues to do with the well-being of the creatures during and after the investigation itself.

Where assessment objectives have to be curtailed for logistic, financial or other reasons, it does not follow that the resulting assessments have no value. They might not reflect the entire curriculum, but they can still be meaningful in terms of a subset of that curriculum – as long as we take care to be clear about what that subset is.

Test types and marking

Objective tests

An 'objective test' is a term often used to describe a test that is entirely composed of multiple-choice items that can be unambiguously marked as right or wrong – like those in Figures 3.8 and 3.9 in Chapter 3. Such tests most often focus on assessing subject knowledge, whether in history, geography, music, or any other subject. But they can also be designed to assess skills, for example numeracy skills in mathematics.

Test items are typically allocated one mark each for a correct response and zero for any other response (technically, this is called 'dichotomous' scoring). Marks may, however, be higher for some items if the relative importance of the fact or concept being assessed warrants it.

Pupil performance will result in a total mark for the test as a whole, or a 'percentage correct' score (percentage of items answered correctly if all items are dichotomous, or percentage of total available marks achieved otherwise). A particular advantage of such tests is that they can be easily marked, by a person or a computer. In addition, the likelihood of marking error is theoretically reduced to zero – although lapses in marker concentration, clerical errors in mark recording, errors in software setup, and glitches in response sheet scanning can all have an influence, albeit small, on the accuracy of marking.

Performance assessment tasks

A 'performance assessment task' is the kind of complex practical task described in the previous chapter, in which a pupil essentially answers a stimulus question or two, or responds to one or more key instructions, by engaging in some observed activity. This could be a practical science investigation, a computer-based task or a group discussion task. Performances in complex tasks are often rated using checklists, in which various aspects of performance are listed for observation and recording. Checkboxes are ticked as the pupil works, and additional details are also sometimes added by the observer.

The particular activities that a pupil might be expected to engage in during the task will be included in the checklist: for example, selecting appropriate pieces of apparatus, zeroing a set of weighing scales, recording measurements, or whatever (see Figure 4.1 for a fictitious example of a simple checklist). The checklist might also include specific outcomes of those component activities that could be judged as right or wrong: for example, whether the weighing scales were *correctly* zeroed, whether the required measurement was correct within given limits, whether a calculation was correctly carried out, and so on. Additional information might be added alongside certain items, such as the actual result of the pupil's calculation, if incorrect.

Checklists are relatively easy to produce for complex tasks. The challenge associated with the checklist approach has to do with making sense of the overall result. The totality of checked boxes must be summarised in some way for the assessor to arrive at a meaningful conclusion about the pupil's overall performance in the task, and hence about the pupil's 'investigation skills', 'collaboration skills', ICT skills or whatever (as demonstrated in that one particular task). This is the Achilles heel of checklist-based assessment. It is easy to report whether an individual pupil zeroed the weighing scales accurately, and what proportion of a group of pupils did the same. It is less easy to make meaningful statements about the pupil's *overall* performance in the task, and often difficult, even impossible, to generalise that performance in that one task to something broader.

Selected appropriate apparatus ☐

Attempted to zero the weighing scales ☐

Zeroed the weighing scales satisfactorily ☐

Measured 1st weight accurately (+/– 0.5 gms) ☐

Drained off liquid ☐

Measured 2nd weight accurately (+/– 0.5 gms) ☐

Subtracted weights ☐

Subtracted weights correctly ☐

Offered a conclusion ☐

Conclusion appropriate ☐

Observer comments:

Figure 4.1 A simple observer checklist

Complex performance tasks can alternatively be numerically marked. Some of the marking can be quite objective, such as giving two marks for accurate measuring of a liquid in the course of a science investigation. Or a degree of assessor judgement will be involved (as is the case for open-ended written tasks), such as when an observer must decide how many marks out of three to award a pupil when he or she successfully saves a file towards the end of an ICT assessment.

This kind of marking is 'analytic', which means that elements in a performance are individually marked, according to some given marking or rating scheme, and the marks then summed up to produce a global mark for the whole performance.

A challenge in this situation is to ensure that the mark distribution across the various elements, as determined by the rating scheme, is appropriate, in terms of the objectives of the whole assessment. Whether accurate measuring of a liquid is worth two marks, one mark, or three or more marks, will depend on the task developer's views about relative worth compared with the other activities involved in the task. This mark 'tariff' issue is an important one, because it dictates the degree to which the performance rating as a whole reflects the underlying assessment intention – differential mark allocations to different aspects of the overall performance in practice reflect what is being more or less valued within the overall ability or skill that is being assessed, whether this is 'investigation skills', 'ICT skills', or 'talking ability'.

Where tasks do not lend themselves to this type of detailed marking, or where the task developer has reason not to favour it, then the alternative is to mark by 'impression'. For example, assessors might award a mark on a 1–5, 0–7 or some other discrete-valued scale, to reflect their judgements about the pupil's global performance, or a product's overall quality. Alternatively, the assessor might be required to use a rating scheme that does not involve mark allocation. It could simply display a set of verbal descriptions that 'define' each of a number of hierarchically ordered 'levels of performance', as illustrated in Table 4.2. The assessor selects the level that most closely matches the pupil's performance, thus making a 'best fit' judgement.

The outcome in such cases would be a number or letter, simply indicating a classification judgement. As a class teacher you will be very familiar with this kind of assessment, especially if you are involved in statutory assessment in the UK.

Other test types

Between these extremes are a variety of different types of test. Think of a typical reading comprehension test, which might equally be considered a structured assessment task, in which a source text, or set of texts, is followed by a series of questions, often grouped into sections by item format. We looked at example items in Chapter 3, based on a source text about young Jason setting off with his little dog in his rowing boat and eventually getting into difficulty. Suppose the text is the one shown in Figure 4.2, which could be suitable for Year 4.

Many alternative comprehension tests could be created on the basis of this short story. The 15-mark test in Figure 4.3, for example, has two sections. Section A includes a set of

---

Table 4.2 Level descriptors for writing assessment

Level 1

Pupils' writing communicates meaning through simple words and phrases. In their reading or their writing, pupils begin to show awareness of how full stops are used. Letters are usually clearly shaped and correctly orientated.

Level 2

Pupils' writing communicates meaning in both narrative and non-narrative forms, using appropriate and interesting vocabulary, and showing some awareness of the reader. Ideas are developed in a sequence of sentences, sometimes demarcated by capital letters and full stops. Simple, monosyllabic words are usually spelt correctly, and where there are inaccuracies the alternative is phonetically plausible. In handwriting, letters are accurately formed and consistent in size.

Level 3

Pupils' writing is often organised, imaginative and clear. The main features of different forms of writing are used appropriately, beginning to be adapted to different readers. Sequences of sentences extend ideas logically and words are chosen for variety and interest. The basic grammatical structure of sentences is usually correct. Spelling is usually accurate, including that of common, polysyllabic words. Punctuation to mark sentences – full stops, capital letters and question marks – is used accurately. Handwriting is joined and legible.

Source: DfEE/QCA 1999a: 59–60

Jason's adventure

It was school holidays, and Jason woke up to a beautiful day. The sun was shining and the sea was calm. He decided it was a perfect day for taking his little dog Megan out with him in his rowing boat. Megan liked going in the boat as much as he did himself. They set off around 2 o'clock in the afternoon. After rowing just a little way from the shore, Jason rested his oars to enjoy the peace and quiet of the sea, as he had done many times before. He was enjoying himself so much that eventually he fell asleep.

But things were to change! Jason didn't know how long he had been asleep, but when he woke up it was to find that the wind was beginning to blow, and his boat was drifting away from the shore. The mist, too, was starting to surround them, and after a while he couldn't see the shore at all any more. He felt anxious, and then he felt afraid, because it was starting to get dark! What was he going to do? Megan, too, was worried. She barked loudly when she saw something suddenly appearing in front of them, looming in the mist. It was an island. Very soon their boat reached the island. They were marooned, but at least they were saved!

Figure 4.2 A fictitious source text for a reading comprehension test

short-answer questions and a sequencing item, while Section B is a summary completion. The four short-answer questions have been given one mark each, the sequencing item is also given one mark, and each of the 10 gaps in the summary completion exercise have a one-mark allocation as well.

Would you say that these mark allocations are appropriate? In particular, would you say that the fourth question in Section A is worth the same number of marks or more marks than any of the first three? There is potentially more information to be retrieved here than in the earlier questions. The first question, for example, simply asks for the name of Jason's little dog, a fact that is found very early on in the text. But in answer to the fourth question pupils could offer one or more of several events, and they have to find these by searching for them towards the end of the text. Here are just a handful of responses that pupils might offer: 'Jason and Megan arrive at an island and get marooned', 'They get marooned', 'They reach an island', 'They were saved', 'Megan barked loudly', 'Jason felt afraid because it was getting dark, and Megan barked. Then an island loomed in the mist and they were marooned' (always recognising that the length of the answer line might preclude a response as long as this). Would all of these responses deserve a mark, and only one mark? What do you think?

Do you think every gap completion in Section B should have the same mark allocation as every other, or would some be worthy of more credit? If they are equally deserving then is one mark per gap the right amount of credit, or should it be half a mark?

These are decisions that the test developer would need to make, and it is these mark allocations that in practice determine how the different skills being assessed in the test are relatively valued.

On a different issue, do you think that including the sequencing item and the summary completion task in the same test might be offering too much help to pupils? Would completing the sequencing item help pupils to do better or worse on the summary completion, or would the partial summary provide too many clues for the sequencing item? If doing one of these will improve performance on the other then it would not be a good idea to include both in the same test. This is true of any kind of test, including objective tests, where each test item is intended in principle to be an independent assessment of the target construct.

Section A

1   What was the name of Jason's little dog?   _____

2   What kind of boat did Jason have?   _____

3   At what time did he set off in his boat?   _____

4   What happened at the end of the story?   _____

_____

These sentences are not in the right order. Show how they *should* be ordered by putting the correct letters in the boxes below.

A   Jason began to feel afraid

B   The boat began to drift from the shore

C   His little dog barked when the island appeared

D   Darkness began to fall

E   Jason set off in his rowing boat

F   The wind got stronger

    1   2   3   4   5   6

Section B

Here is a summary of the story after the wind had started to rise. Fill each gap with one or more words. Use words from the story or your own words.

Jason was _____ being in the boat so much that he eventually

_____ asleep. He woke to find that the _____

was beginning to _____ and mist was _____to

surround them. As the boat drifted _____ and further from

_____ Jason began to feel _____. His little dog

barked _____ when she saw the _____ loom out of

the mist.

Figure 4.3 A possible 15-mark reading comprehension test based on the story in Figure 4.2

For a real example, have a look at the test description in Figure 4.4. The test was used in the 2003 Assessment of Achievement Programme survey of science in Scotland, as part of the assessment of reading as a core skill. The source material in this case is not the usual 'imaginative' text but a set of short factual pieces about friction. The test itself comprises six sections, including two summary completion exercises and two sets of sentence completion items. You will be interested to know that this test, like others of similar type used in the survey, was followed by a related writing task as a seventh test section: children were asked to 'Write a short report on some of the ways that friction affects our lives. Also, think of other everyday examples of how friction affects us' (AAP 2005a: 34). The intention behind the writing task was to assess pupils' writing ability (another 'core skill'), not their science knowledge.

For a different example, think of a science test designed to cover the primary science curriculum for 7–11 year olds. There might be 24 questions in the test, between them equally representing the major areas of science. The questions would probably be structured, each with a selection of item formats to maintain the pupils' interest and motivation as well as to contribute to the assessment objective: 'to assess pupils' science learning at the end of Year 6'.

Unless tests are deliberately controlled at the creation stage, then it frequently happens that different questions carry different total marks, and that the items within each question vary in mark allocation as well. This is evident, for instance, in the National Curriculum tests currently in operation in England (Chapter 6).

Creating tests

When we assess 'learning' what exactly do we think that we are assessing? This is a fundamental question that underpins our development and use of assessment items, tasks and tests. It is relatively straightforward to create a single test item to match a single specific assessment objective. Thus, if we want to find out if children know how many legs a spider has we can simply ask them orally, get them to respond to a multiple-choice question like the one in Figure 3.5 in Chapter 3, or ask them to draw a spider or, more efficiently, have them sketch the legs on a legless spider drawing, as in the other item in Figure 3.5 in Chapter 3. Similarly, if we want to find out whether a pupil has mastered the skill of adding two-digit numbers then we can quickly find out by asking the child to carry out some relevant 'sums'.

A 400-word text explains what friction is, gives everyday examples of its effects, and discusses the value of engine lubrication. Six sections of test items follow, presenting 20 items in total:

- Section A invites pupils to circle three correct descriptions of friction from among six possibilities
- Section B invites pupils to give two examples from the text where friction was helpful and two where friction caused problems
- Section C is a summary completion
- Section D comprises sentence completion items
- Section E is a summary completion
- Section F comprises sentence completion items.

Figure 4.4 A reading comprehension task based on text-based information about friction (Source: AAP 2005a: 34)

But what if we want to assess a child's learning on an entire curriculum? We could not possibly create the time that would be needed to test everything in that curriculum at one time, say at the end of the school year. And even if we could take the hours that it would need at the expense of teaching time, it would be at risk of exhausting the children with the volume of testing they would have to endure, so that they might eventually rebel if not drift into a catatonic state (as you might do yourself as you supervise the assessment for hours on end). Whether you are creating your own summative test or using someone else's, the test will inevitably include only some of the curriculum topics but not all, and will include some of the knowledge and skills embodied in the curriculum, but not all. How does a test developer ensure that the test appropriately covers the curriculum, even though this must inevitably be sampled? The answer is that the test developer would use a 'test specification'.

Test specification

A test specification outlines the structure and composition of an intended test. The specification might be one-dimensional, as in the example in Table 4.3 for numeracy, which simply indicates how many items are to be included in the test to represent each relevant skill. Or it might be two-dimensional, as in Table 4.4, in which item format has also been factored in.

Test specifications can be more complex than either of these, depending on the number of important curriculum features that need to be taken into account and appropriately reflected in the test. Test length, though, will constrain possibilities. The shorter a test is to be in terms of the number of items it is to contain, or equivalently in terms of the amount of time it is allowed to 'steal' from normal class teaching time, the less flexibility a test developer will have in controlling content to meet a demanding test specification.

Bloom's taxonomy

There are occasions when specific learning objectives are difficult to identify within a given programme of study, or where the tests to be created are not intended to be linked directly to any particular curriculum. The tests used in some international attainment surveys (Chapter 7) are examples. In such cases, test developers need a different approach in order to specify their tests.

Table 4.3 An example specification for a 24-item numeracy test

Skill	No. items
Addition	2
Subtraction	2
Multiplication	2
Division	2
Percentages	3
Decimals	3
Rounding	2
Fractions	4
Chart completion	4
Total items	24

Table 4.4 An example two-dimensional specification for a 24-item numeracy test

Skill	Multiple choice	Short answer	Total items
Addition	1	1	2
Subtraction	1	1	2
Multiplication	1	1	2
Division	1	1	2
Percentages	1	2	3
Decimals	1	2	3
Rounding	0	2	2
Fractions	1	3	4
Chart completion	2	2	4
Total items	9	15	24

Several decades ago, Benjamin Bloom and colleagues asked themselves the question 'What are we trying to assess?', and eventually came up with a classification of learning, known as 'Bloom's taxonomy' (Bloom *et al.* 1956). The taxonomy was 'a framework for classifying statements of what we expect or intend students to learn as a result of instruction' (Krathwohl 2002: 212). It was inspired by a perceived need to rationalise (multiple-choice) item development in the United States, by providing an item classification system that would facilitate the rapid creation of item banks through the sharing of pre-classified test items among higher education institutions (an item bank simply being a large collection of test items, from which items could be drawn as needed to create tests).

The 1956 publication focused on the cognitive (knowledge-based) domain. But work had also been underway to establish a corresponding taxonomy in the affective (attitudinal) and psychomotor (skills-based) domains. The resulting affective domain taxonomy was published almost ten years later (Krathwohl *et al.* 1964). A taxonomy for the psychomotor domain was unfortunately never published by the original taxonomy development group.

Each domain was described in terms of a hierarchy of levels of learning development. For the cognitive domain six hierarchical levels were identified (the taxonomy embodies several subdivisions within each level):

- Evaluation (highest level)
- Synthesis
- Analysis
- Application
- Comprehension
- Knowledge (lowest level).

The bottom three levels are the ones that are most used in the assessment of school-age children, both for constructing test items and larger tasks, and for structuring tests. However, while it's interesting, and sometimes necessary, to try to classify test items against these apparently distinguishable characteristics, it isn't always easy to do this successfully. This is because one pupil's demonstration of 'knowledge' will be another pupil's demonstration of 'application', and so on. Think of a phonic decoding test, in which some of the real words might already be familiar on sight to some pupils, who would be using recall to pronounce the word correctly, but unfamiliar to others, who would have to apply their learned decoding skills to arrive at the same end (satisfying the intention behind the test).

Or consider an item in science that is in principle intended to have a pupil apply understanding of a particular science concept in order to predict or explain some phenomenon, like evaporation being the reason why a water spill disappeared over minutes as though by magic. Some pupils might indeed apply their conceptual understanding of evaporation to respond to the question, but others might simply regurgitate a learned response to this specific example.

If taxonomies are to serve a useful purpose in test construction, as they undoubtedly can do, the location of items within them demands consensus from several independent reviewers, with different types of teaching experience with different kinds of pupils.

Bloom's original taxonomy is now well over 50 years old, and yet it is still widely used in test development, albeit in various revised, adapted or otherwise modified forms. In an effort to address the issue of classification ambiguity, a recent important revision of the taxonomy took place in the late 1990s, with the new revised taxonomy published in the early 2000s (Anderson, Krathwohl *et al.* 2001; for a useful overview see Krathwohl 2002). The cognitive process levels in the new taxonomy are:

- Creating
- Evaluating
- Analysing
- Applying
- Understanding
- Remembering (lowest level, previously labelled 'knowledge').

Note that the level labels in the original taxonomy have been changed from nouns to verbs, a small modification perhaps, but an important one intended to make the taxonomy more 'user-friendly': 'one criterion for selecting category labels was the use of terms that teachers use in talking about their work' (Krathwohl 2002: 214). In addition, the two top levels in the original taxonomy have been switched, with the old 'synthesis' being renamed 'creating'. Reading the new taxonomy from its lowest level upwards, here are more detailed descriptions of the intended meanings of the short labels:

- **Remembering**: Retrieving, recognizing, and recalling relevant knowledge from long-term memory.
- **Understanding**: Constructing meaning from oral, written, and graphic messages through interpreting, exemplifying, classifying, summarizing, inferring, comparing, and explaining.
- **Applying**: Carrying out or using a procedure through executing, or implementing.
- **Analyzing**: Breaking material into constituent parts, determining how the parts relate to one another and to an overall structure or purpose through differentiating, organizing, and attributing.
- **Evaluating**: Making judgments based on criteria and standards through checking and critiquing.
- **Creating**: Putting elements together to form a coherent or functional whole; reorganizing elements into a new pattern or structure through generating, planning, or producing.

Anderson, Krathwohl *et al.* 2001: 67–8

A more striking feature of the taxonomy revision is a structural change that replaced the original one-dimensional six-level structure with a two-dimensional schema. This was achieved by adding a 'knowledge dimension' to the existing, slightly revised, 'process dimension'. Four knowledge levels were identified: factual, conceptual, procedural and meta-cognitive, by extracting, rearranging and extending the subdivisions of the 'knowledge' level in the original 1956 taxonomy.

The resulting two-dimensional grid, known as the 'taxonomy table', therefore comprises 24 cells (six process levels by four knowledge levels) as a top layer (see Figure 4.5). Since each process level and each knowledge level is further subdivided there are actually many more possibilities than this for classifying learning and assessment objectives and in turn test items. 'Remembering', for instance, is subdivided into 'recognise' and 'recall' (from long-term memory), while 'factual knowledge' is subdivided into 'knowledge of terminology' and 'knowledge of specific details and elements'.

The grid is a useful practical tool for describing courses and units in terms of their intended teaching/learning objectives, and for analysing classroom activities to gauge the match between intended objectives and achieved objectives. In assessment the grid can be invaluable for guiding item development, for post-classifying pre-existing items, for monitoring the composition of a continually growing item bank, and for creating tests to pre-defined specifications.

Note, however, one important point about the revised taxonomy table, which potentially, if marginally, limits its application potential. This is that the revised taxonomy, like the original, was developed for use in a context in which 'objective testing' was the predominant form of assessment – it is only a decade or so ago that 'alternative assessment' emerged in the United States as the generic term for assessment using any form of test item other than multiple-choice. This means that further useful modifications might yet be made to the taxonomy as

Process	Knowledge			
	Factual	Conceptual	Procedural	Meta-cognitive
Remember				
Understand				
Apply				
Analyse				
Evaluate				
Create				

Figure 4.5 Revised cognitive domain taxonomy table (adapted from Krathwohl 2002)

currently defined, in order to embrace the wider variety of assessment items and tasks that actually exist.

Interpreting test scores

Suppose in a science test a pupil scores 20 marks out of a maximum possible total of 24, or 83 per cent. What can you infer from this result? It's a high score, but perhaps all the pupils got high scores. What does this one result actually tell you about the pupil's 'science ability'? It might tell you one of two things: where the pupil stands in relation to other pupils who took the same or an equivalent test, or, alternatively, what it is that the pupil actually knows and can do in science (however 'science' is defined). Tests which offer the first kind of interpretation are called 'norm-referenced'. Tests which purport to offer the second kind of information are called 'criterion-referenced'. Whichever type of test is being constructed will determine the criteria that will be applied when pretested items are considered for test inclusion.

Norm-referencing

Let's start with norm-referencing. The term 'norm-referencing' describes use of a test to rank pupils as efficiently as possible, usually, but not always, for a selection purpose. We might, for example, simply want to identify the top 10 per cent of pupils in the class, in the school, in the authority or in the country, in terms of their science ability, their numeracy skills or their history knowledge. Or we might need to identify several groups of pupils, ordered by their test attainments: say the top 10 per cent, the next 20 per cent, the 'middle' 50 per cent and the bottom 20 per cent. A test that serves these kinds of purpose best will be a test that spreads pupils as much as possible along the test score scale. In other words, the test would need to have high 'discrimination' properties.

Imagine a chart – histogram or line chart – that illustrates the distribution of pupils' total marks on a test whose maximum mark is 16. If all the pupils do very badly on the test then their scores will all be clustered towards the bottom end of the asymmetric distribution: the distribution would be 'right-skewed', meaning that it would have a long tail on the right and a peak to the left (as for Test A in Figure 4.6). If all pupils do well on the test then the reverse will be the case: the distribution would be 'left-skewed', meaning a tail on the left and a peak on the right (Test C in Figure 4.6). A test which more evenly spreads pupils will produce a symmetrical distribution (like Test B in Figure 4.6). Usually the best test distribution for a norm-referenced application is a 'flat' symmetric distribution that spreads pupils relatively evenly across the whole mark scale.

The best way to create a well-functioning norm-referenced test is to ensure that all the test items within it are themselves maximally discriminating. So we would not want to include items that almost every pupil would get right or that almost every pupil would get wrong. Very easy and very hard items would not be useful, because they would not contribute to spreading pupils on the scale. Conventionally, when judging the utility of multiple-choice items, we look for items that between around 30 per cent and 70 per cent of pupils would get right, which we find out by pretesting the items with samples of pupils (300 or so) of the same general type as those the test is ultimately intended to be used with (such as Year 6 pupils in England from a range of social backgrounds and school types). The proportion of pupils who get a multiple-choice item right is called its 'facility'.

But we also want to be sure that all the items in the test are assessing the same 'construct', i.e. the same ability (as in 'reading comprehension') or the same set of related skills (such as

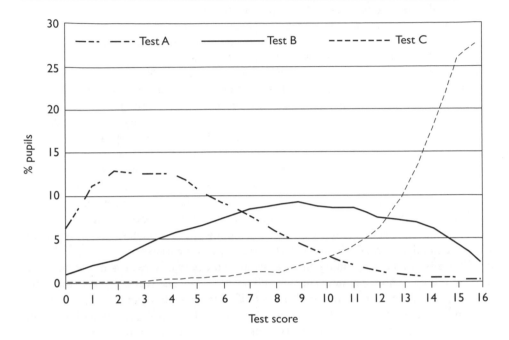

Figure 4.6 Score distributions for three 16-item tests

in 'numeracy'). In other words, we would be looking for items that 'hang together' empirically, so that if a pupil gets one of the items right then the chances are the pupil would get the other ones right as well (unfortunately, nothing is so predictable in pupil assessment that we can say with certainty which items particular pupils will get right or wrong). And so we also look at the item's discriminating power, the way the item behaves with respect to the collective behaviour of all the other items in the test. Technically, we use the item's correlation with the rest of the test as a measure of its 'discrimination'. Correlation coefficients, which always range from −1 to +1, crop up all the time in educational measurement; we shall meet them again in connection with validity and reliability measures in the next chapter. When used as indices of discrimination, correlations of 0.3 or more are typically employed to screen items for inclusion in tests intended for norm-referenced uses.

'Standardised tests' are norm-referenced tests whose individual pupil results can be converted into an age-related 'norm', such as 'reading age'. Such norms are produced during standardisation exercises, in which the test is administered to large representative samples of pupils, if not to the entire cohort at some point in time. The test score distributions of bands of pupils within particular age ranges are standardised, i.e. statistically transformed, so that they have a particular mean and standard deviation (for example, 100 and 15). An individual test score indicates whether the pupil is average, or above or below average for his or her age, in terms of reading ability or whatever other construct the test is ostensibly assessing. Then when the test is used by a class teacher anywhere in the country the teacher will know which pupils are reading above or below average for their age, and how the class as a whole is doing.

Standardised tests need periodically to be restandardised, not only because an entire population can improve abilities and skills in certain areas over a period of time but also because fixed tests can become dated or over-practised. If you are using a standardised test in your school be sure to find out when and how it was last standardised.

'Computer-adaptive assessment' (van der Linden and Glas 2000; Wainer 2000), also known as 'tailored testing' or 'personalised assessment', is another form of norm-referenced testing, this time based on an application of 'item response theory' (IRT). Practical application of IRT involves quite complicated 'black box' manipulations of the original test data, so that the relationship of test scores into transformed 'scale scores' can appear quite obscure to the untrained observer (which includes the general public); if you are mathematically-minded you will find a relatively painless introduction to IRT in Hambleton *et al.* (1991). IRT differs from the assessment models we have assumed up until now, in the sense that whereas traditionally pupils would all take the same, usually paper-based, norm-referenced test, in this application every pupil can in practice take a different test from every other.

Each pupil starts the computer-based test by attempting one or more test items. Depending on whether a pupil answers the items correctly or not a second, easier or more difficult, item or set of items is offered. Depending on the answers to the previous items a third item choice is made, and so on. With fewer items than would be needed in a conventional test, the pupils can be given an appropriate 'scale score' and classified into an attainment band.

The items posed to pupils are drawn from a large item bank, in which, in addition to the usual curriculum-style classifications, every item has empirical properties attached to it that are estimated through large-scale pretesting. An essential property is the item's 'difficulty', but discrimination, too, can feature, depending on the IRT model being used. This style of testing sounds ideal – computer-based and in principle efficient. But how well it lives up to expectations depends on the degree to which a very strong assumption underpinning the IRT model is met. This is that item 'difficulties' do not change, either from one pupil group to another, from one pupil to another, or over a period of time.

Criterion-referencing

Criterion-referencing is the term used to identify whether a pupil has achieved some given goal, rather than to know where that pupil is with respect to other pupils of similar type and age. At its simplest an item can function as a criterion-referencing assessment tool, the pupil's response immediately providing evidence that he or she has acquired a piece of knowledge, understood a particular concept or mastered a specific skill. So we can ask how many legs insects have, what the Romans used for road foundations, how much liquid a given tumbler holds to its brim (requiring practical measurement for a response), how many children share 20 sweets if they end up with four sweets each, and so on, and find out whether pupils have met the teaching and learning objective reflected in the assessment criterion. Always recognising, of course, that a child might provide the correct response one day and an entirely different response the next!

When a test must sample an entire curriculum, criterion-referencing takes the form of 'domain-referencing'. The curriculum domain, which might be the Year 6 history programme of study, say, or the early primary English curriculum, is represented by the collection of items in the test, which in turn might be drawn from a larger pool or bank of relevant items using a given test specification.

Average or total test scores, for individual pupils or for pupil groups, such as boys and girls, reflect performance on the test. These are generalised to indicate performance on the entire domain. We can then use test scores, the surrogate domain scores, to compare the performance of different pupil subgroups, and of pupils in general from one test session to another (perhaps one survey to another in large-scale attainment survey programmes).

Pre-determined cut scores are typically used to categorise pupils into various achievement groups or bands, suitably labelled. For example, a pupil might need to respond correctly to two-thirds of the items in an objective test, or to achieve two-thirds of the marks in a test featuring more varied item formats, to be considered to have shown sufficiently good performance on the test to warrant a judgement of 'secure attainment' on the underpinning subject domain.

Dual referencing

The tests used in National Curriculum assessment in England at the end of key stage 2 (end of primary) are based on the whole programme of study for that key stage, which spans four school years (see Chapter 6). But pupils are classified into attainment levels, on the basis of teacher judgement and separately on the basis of the tests. Teachers use 'level descriptors' (Appendix 2) when arriving at 'best fit' level judgements for each of their pupils, i.e. they are expected to adopt a criterion-referenced approach to 'levelling' their pupils. The tests, though, have not been designed to do the same thing. The tests sample each programme of study, and span more than one level. So a way had to be found to convert test score distributions into bands to permit the level classification of pupils. How was this to be done?

The strategy adopted was to follow the practice of the qualifications awarding bodies that deliver grade awards for the different subject examinations taken by pupils at 16+ (General Certificate of Secondary Education – GCSE) and at 18 (General Certificate of Education – GCE): for technical accounts of the very complex procedures used see, for example, Cresswell 1994, Morrison, *et al.* 1994, Bramley 2006. Statisticians identify potential 'level thresholds', or 'cut scores', for the current year's test in a subject (science, say), on the basis of the previous year's cut scores and comparisons of the respective proportions of pupils who would be classified in a particular way if that cut score were to be reused. Subject specialists then scrutinise scripts around the proposed cut scores, making judgements as best they can about the standards of performance of current year pupils compared with those of the previous year. In this way decisions emerge about the most appropriate cut scores, or 'level thresholds', with which to classify pupils into attainment levels (see QCA 2007 and Newton 2009 for further detail).

This practice supposedly carries each 'level standard' across years, in principle enabling statements to be made about the attainments of the current year's cohort in isolation and when compared with previous cohorts (over-time monitoring – see Chapter 7). There are many problems with this strategy, however, not least of which is the possibility of 'standards drift' (this is where examiners tend to give the current cohort 'benefit of the doubt' by going for the lower of two threshold choices for a particular level). As a result, several commentators have questioned the validity of the apparent (upward) attainment trends that emerged in the early years (for example, Tymms 2004, Tymms and Merrell 2007).

In addition to this form of pseudo-criterion-referenced reporting, the results of the same National Curriculum tests are simultaneously given norm-referenced interpretations. Pupils' test results are fed back to schools in raw form (i.e. untransformed test scores), and schools are given tables with which they can convert each pupil's raw score in each subject into an age-standardised score (QCA 2007).

Questions for reflection

*   Look back at the items shown in Chapter 3, and see where you think they slot into the taxonomy table in Figure 4.5. Find a colleague willing to do the same exercise independently (without having to read either chapter beforehand!), and then compare your results. How would you explain any differences in your judgements?
*   In general pupils learn most of what they know about a subject from their learning in school. But they can also learn outside school, from play and exploration, from books, from the television, from the internet, and from family and friends. To what extent do you think this out-of-school learning differs from one pupil to another, and from one subject to another? How often would such differences muddy attempts to categorise items using the taxonomy table?
*   How likely is it that an item would be slotted into the same place in the taxonomy table depending on the age of the pupils responding to it? Would any particular type of item be stable in this sense?
*   Have a look at a test that you use, or have used, in your school. It could be a teacher-made test, a commercial standardised test, a National Curriculum test, or any other test. What can you say about the composition of the test? And how well-matched would you say the composition is to the test's intended assessment purpose?

Further reading

Anderson, P. and Morgan, G. (2008) *Developing Tests and Questionnaires for a National Assessment of Educational Achievement*. Washington: The World Bank.

Krathwohl, D. R. (2002) 'A Revision of Bloom's Taxonomy: An overview', *Theory into Practice*, 41: 212–18.

Tymms, P. and Merrell, C. (2007) *Standards and Quality in English Primary Schools Over Time: The National Evidence Research Survey 4/1*, London: Esmée Fairbairn Foundation.

Chapter 5

Assuring quality in assessment

How do you judge how good an assessment instrument is? How is assessment quality defined? What is the meaning of assessment 'validity' and assessment 'reliability', and what roles do these play in assuring assessment quality? What are some of the threats to validity and reliability? When the assessment instrument is not a test or task but is the class teacher, how do we explore the quality of pupil assessment? Chapter 5 addresses such questions, looking in particular at the following:

* Dependability – validity plus reliability
* Assessment validity
* Assessment reliability
* The special case of teacher assessment.

Dependability – validity plus reliability

'Validity' and 'reliability' are the two most important concepts in assessment. Together they determine the quality, the 'dependability', and in turn the value, the usefulness, of assessments, whether of knowledge, understanding, skill or attitude.

What we assess should be as close as possible to what we intend to assess, if we are to have validity in assessment. And our assessment result needs to be as close to 'the truth' as we can manage, however the truth is defined, if we are to have assessment reliability. Whether we are literally measuring how much of an attribute a pupil possesses – for example, historical knowledge, numeracy ability or a cooperative attitude – or discretely classifying the pupil in some way – such as being a 'level 3 reader', 'having little sense of community' or, in writing, 'demonstrating audience awareness' – there will usually be some uncertainty attached to that measurement or classification. This is true even when the attribute or property being measured is well-defined, and can be measured directly, like a child's height or weight.

When school nurses measure pupils' weights they are measuring a property that is tangible and easily defined. Despite that, while the weight will normally be measured well enough, it is unlikely to be measured perfectly, even with the best weighing machine the school or authority can afford. This is because human beings are not inanimate objects. Some children are unable to stand still, no matter how many times they are asked to try to do so. And the more they move about on the weighing scales the more the weight reading will fluctuate. How carefully the nurse sets out to measure a pupil's weight will depend partly on the purpose for which the information is required. For some purposes a weight measurement to the nearest half kilo could be more than sufficient, while for other purposes greater precision might be necessary. The more important the purpose of the measurement the more care the nurse would need to take to produce a dependable result. Despite all the care taken to 'standardise' the measurement procedure, however, different readings could result each time a pupil's weight is measured, even though the weight itself has not changed in the seconds between readings. For this reason, the nurse might weigh the pupil several times, before averaging the readings to arrive as close as possible to 'the truth', i.e. to the child's actual weight at that moment in time.

So it is with educational assessment. Except that the challenges of quality assessment are greater in this context. This is partly because, as noted earlier, even when we have a clear definition to work with, the knowledge, understanding, skill or attitude being assessed cannot always be directly measured, as weight can. To find out what individual pupils know or can do in geography or mathematics, or what they think about the importance of these subjects for their future lives, we have to ask them questions or give them tasks to do, and then judge their answers and performances in some way to produce a 'measurement' or classification.

'Validity' is to do with the 'what' and the 'how' of assessment, while reliability has to do with the 'how well'. It is sometimes useful to use a target analogy to understand the difference between the two concepts (see Figure 5.1).

Validity is about being 'on target'. The more on target we can be, in the sense of devising an assessment instrument that faithfully focuses on those abilities or skills that we intend to measure, the more accurate, the more valid, will be our assessments. If we intend to assess whether a child can add and subtract 2-digit numbers, then we would want to be sure we included both addition and subtraction questions involving 2-digit numbers in our test in roughly equal numbers. We would not want to have a greater emphasis on addition, say, than subtraction. And we certainly would not want to introduce multiplication, division or any other numeracy skills into the mix.

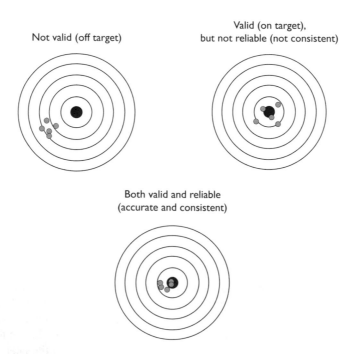

Figure 5.1 Validity (accuracy) and reliability (consistency)

On a broader scale, if we were setting out to assess the totality of a pupil's science learning by Year 6, then we would probably want our assessment to cover investigation skills as well as factual knowledge and conceptual understanding. If the assessment falls short of our intention in any sense, if its results are 'off target', then validity is lost.

Assessment reliability is not about being on or off target. Reliability is about consistency, or repeatability. If we were to assess the same pupil more than once with our test (something which would not be a meaningful activity in practice – but more on this later) then reliability is concerned with how much or how little variation there would be in the results. Where validity is about accuracy, reliability is about precision.

To a great extent assessment validity can be assured before a test is created and used. It can be built-in at the design stage, by developing and using a 'test specification' as discussed in Chapter 4. This is true to a much lesser extent for assessment reliability, which is a more technical concept that can only be established through analysis of the empirical results of the assessment process, that is, through analysis of the pupils' test scores or classifications. Reliability is a property of test scores not of the test itself.

This chapter begins by looking further at the concept of validity, with reliability brought into the picture later.

Assessment validity

Assessment 'validity' is in principle a simple concept. It is essentially about how well an assessment instrument or procedure measures what it is intended to measure. It is concerned with how appropriately we reflect the knowledge, understanding, skill, personality trait or attitude that we intend to assess, both in the assessment tools that we use and, equally importantly, in the assessment criteria that we apply to children's responses and behaviours. To assure validity in our assessments we need to make sure that the questions we ask children about their learning, the tasks we give them to do during their assessment, and the observations we make of them as they work, are relevant in terms of the learning objectives whose achievement we are trying to assess. And we also need to ensure that the way in which we allocate credit to item responses and to the different aspects of a practical performance is consistent with our assessment intentions.

Face validity and content validity

A number of different types of assessment validity have been identified and proposed (Messick 1989 is a standard reference). Among them, the principal types that the primary teacher needs to be directly concerned with are 'face validity' and its more formal relation 'content validity'.

'Face validity' is the simplest possible validity concept. It refers to the degree to which an assessment instrument 'looks the part'. It is based on an intuitive judgement about what an item, test, questionnaire or group activity *appears* to measure.

If we create a test of our pupils' learning of number skills, for example, then, provided the pupils had been taught all four operations, we would want to include examples of addition, subtraction, multiplication and division in the test, and not just addition and subtraction. The items would also need to be appropriate for the age group concerned – if we were assessing eight-year-olds then the items should feature only single-digit or double-digit numbers. Provided these conditions were met, and provided the four operations were represented equally, or in some intentionally unequal way, the test would have face validity.

The same principles apply to questionnaires that are designed to assess attitudes and other personal characteristics. In an enquiry focusing on motivation to learn mathematics, for instance, we would expect to see relevant questions about this subject: perhaps statements about mathematics that pupils are invited to indicate their level of agreement with, such as 'Our maths lessons are very interesting' or 'Mathematics is really important for jobs'. We would not expect to see a focus on history or French – a question or two comparing these with mathematics might be acceptable, but nothing more. And clearly all the questions or statements would need to be considered acceptable as addressing the underlying focus of interest, which is motivation to learn mathematics.

Whether test items are to be used as stand-alone learning checks or as elements in a test their face validity should also be checked, however 'atomistic' the items might be. We can use the minibeasts example again here. If we wanted to find out whether our class of pupils had grasped the important distinguishing feature of insects that we had set out to teach them, i.e. that insects have six legs and not four or eight or any other number, then we would ask a question that focuses on this specific fact. The question shown in Figure 2.1 in Chapter 2 is just such a question (which of six pictured minibeasts are insects?). At first sight, this looks like an appropriate item for testing whether children can distinguish insects from other minibeasts by virtue of their number of legs. It seems to have face validity. But is the item actually assessing what we think it is?

Of the six pictures of minibeasts in the item – snail, spider, bee, fly, worm and caterpillar – only the fly and the bee have six legs. But if a pupil correctly answered the question, by checking the boxes against the fly and the bee, and only those boxes, could we be sure that this would be evidence that the pupil had in fact learned that minibeasts are insects if they have six legs and not any other number? Is it not possible that the pupil might simply have learned from the teacher that flies and bees are insects, and that worms, spiders, centipedes and snails are not, without necessarily having grasped the underlying classification criterion, in the same way that pupils taught reading using the 'look and say' approach learn how to pronounce whole words without necessarily acquiring the phonic decoding skills to work out the correct pronunciation themselves?

A better, but less 'authentic' item, could present the pupil with a set of unrecognisable minibeasts, in the form of featureless 'bodies' with different numbers of 'legs' – sketches of the kind very young children might draw – and then ask which of the minibeasts were insects. Alternatively the pupil could simply be asked 'How many legs does an insect have?' or 'A minibeast that we haven't seen before has a round body and ten legs. Is it an insect?' perhaps followed by 'Why do you think it [is or isn't] an insect?'.

A second example will illustrate the issue even more clearly. In Figure 5.2 we see a very similar test question. This time pupils are asked to identify which three of the six animals are birds (note the guidance given to pupils in this example that alerts them to the fact that exactly three boxes should be checked, unlike the minibeasts example, where no such scaffolding is included). The pupils are expected to know that what distinguishes birds from other animals is the fact that they have feathers. It is not that they can fly, like the bat (which is included precisely to look for evidence of that misconception, for diagnostic interest). But the drawings in the item are too small to show feathers (even blown up to the size actually presented to pupils it is impossible to see feathers).

The only way that pupils could get this item correct would be to know beforehand that owls, penguins and swans all have feathers and so must be birds, or simply that swans and penguins as well as owls *are* birds, with feathers not a consideration. So, when pupils answer this question correctly we cannot necessarily infer the reason. Is it because they have applied

Tick (✓) the three **drawings** that show **birds**

A □   B □   C □

D □   E □   F □

Figure 5.2 A bird identification task (Source: AAP 2005a: 10)

their knowledge that penguins, swans and owls all have feathers, while dogs, tortoises and bats do not, and that creatures with feathers are birds – the intention behind the item? Or have they simply learned which of several creatures they studied in class are birds and which are not, for whatever reason, and are simply recalling that information (the lowest level in Bloom's taxonomy of learning – see Chapter 4)? In either case, the item would be tapping science knowledge and understanding, but the specific type of knowledge being demonstrated could be different for different pupils. The item's validity for testing a piece of animal classification knowledge would have to be in doubt.

To remove the doubt about assessment validity the question could be expanded and in a second part pupils could be asked why they made their particular choices, recognising, of course, that some pupils might simply reply 'because they're birds'! If a pupil made a wrong selection that included two birds and the bat then this would tell us that the pupil definitely did not have the right concept about bird classification, recognising birds, sometimes wrongly, as creatures with 'wings' that fly. Or maybe it simply tells us that these pupils, like many others, were pretty sure about owls and swans, perhaps through greater familiarity with these particular birds in pictures and in real life, and since they needed a third 'bird' to make the required set, then having easily eliminated the dog and tortoise, they chose the bat.

Content validity is closely related to face validity. It is about content relevance and, in the case of tests, curriculum coverage. To give an example, it would probably be important that a written primary science test not only includes topics from across the relevant science curriculum, something that could be judged superficially, but also that a) there should be a balance between 'life processes and living things', 'materials and their properties' and 'physical processes', and b) that different topics within each area should be given relative prominence in terms of their importance within the curriculum.

Similarly, if we are assessing the mathematics learned by children over a four-year programme, then we would want our assessment to cover as much of the whole curriculum as possible in an appropriately representative way. We would want to see questions tapping number skills, fraction problems, data handling tasks, and mental mathematics, but without an overemphasis on any particular topic with respect to the curriculum.

After the event, content validity can be formally evaluated by mapping the test's composition against an appropriate curriculum grid or taxonomy table, as described in Chapter 4. To assure content validity *before* a test is constructed a 'test specification' should be drawn up to reflect the test's intended curriculum representation, and test items selected to meet that specification. Tables 4.3 and 4.4 in Chapter 4 offer example test specifications for a 24-item numeracy test. For another example, we can think of a 45-minute science knowledge test for which the test specification might require eight multi-part questions from each of the three science areas, with at least one but not more than two questions on any particular topic within each area.

Construct validity

Construct validity is the degree to which an assessment instrument or procedure elicits evidence of the particular knowledge, skill or attitude – the construct – that is in principle being assessed. Several examples of constructs have already been mentioned here and in earlier chapters: for example, 'reading comprehension', 'numeracy', 'cooperative skills', 'mental mathematics', 'self-confidence', 'sense of community', 'motivation to learn'. Other examples include 'writing ability', 'science investigation skills', 'perseverance', 'historical knowledge', 'creative ability' and 'attitude to mathematics'. You will be able to think of many more.

We can use numeracy again to begin to explore the concept of construct validity. We know that we want pupils not only to learn the basic number skills but also to be able to apply those skills in different contexts. We equally want to motivate them to do their best in assessments. And so in addition to testing whether pupils can add and subtract in the abstract, for example with questions (actually instructions) like 'Add 5 and 15', we usually want to see if they can do the same calculations in word problems, such as 'Jessica has found five ladybirds in the garden and her brother Daniel has found 15. How many ladybirds do they have altogether?'.

Word problems add 'authenticity' to numeracy assessment, setting calculations in familiar contexts, giving them a meaningful purpose in a pupil's eyes (or at least that is the theory – we could argue whether counting ladybirds would appear to the majority of Year 1 pupils as having a meaningful purpose!). Equally importantly, they provide you, as the teacher assessor, with opportunities to find out how well pupils can apply their learned skills across the curriculum – the issue of 'skills transfer'.

But a potentially problematic issue here is the extent to which the addition of words means that we are not testing pure number skills but some combination of number skills and reading ability: the dependency on reading ability potentially 'clouds' the assessment of numeracy skill. The greater the dependency on reading – the more words there are and the more complex the language – the more important the clouding is likely to become, and the less trust we will be able to have in our assessment results as measures of number skills.

For another example, we can pick up the item in Figure 3.6 in Chapter 3. This is a chart completion item, with the very simple requirement that pupils add one bar to a bar chart to show that five pupils had birds as pets. In Figure 3.6 the amount of text pupils have to read to find out what they must do is quite reduced. But look at an alternative version of the item, shown in Figure 5.3. Even though the language is still relatively simple, there is quite a lot more of it. Poor readers might baulk at this item before ever finding out how simple the numeracy skill being demanded actually is. Reading ability interferes with the assessment of numeracy ability.

A Year 3 class carried out a survey to find out how many pupils had different kinds of pets. The results are shown in the bar chart, except that the bar for birds is missing. Five children had pet birds. Add this information to the chart.

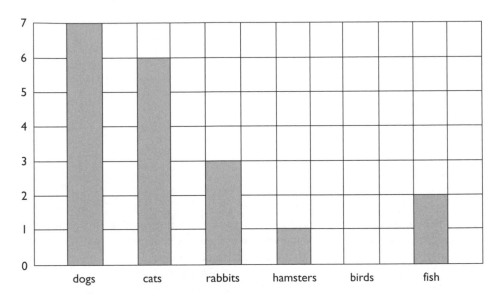

Figure 5.3 Chart completion item with high reading demand

In other types of assessment, writing ability can cloud the assessment of other constructs. Turning to reading comprehension again, look at the question shown in Figure 5.4. The stimulus passage, remember, was a story about Jason, who became marooned on an island when his rowing boat drifted away from the shore (see Chapter 4). The question asks pupils 'Why did Jason feel so afraid as darkness began to fall?', and invites an open-ended written response. Another question with the same format is this one from history: 'How did the Romans build their roads?'. And this one from science: 'Explain why plants need light to survive?'. To what extent, for what proportion of pupils, would you say these items are likely to be assessing what they were intended to assess, that is reading comprehension in the first case, historical knowledge in the second, and science knowledge and understanding in the third, rather than writing ability?

Why do you think an open-ended response format was used in these cases? Could the assessment information that an assessor would be looking for be accessed in any other way, do you think? Maybe by using a multiple-choice format in the first and last case, and a matching item in the second (matching road layers with materials used)? This would eliminate the risk of writing ability interfering with the pupil's ability to demonstrate reading comprehension skills, historical knowledge or scientific understanding. Would anything be lost in order to make the gain? Would assessment validity be improved or reduced?

The more writing a pupil is required to produce, particularly in a pressured situation like a formal test, the more scribbled and the less coherent that writing is likely to be compared with what the pupil might have produced in a day-to-day classroom situation. Moreover, even if pupils could read a story with understanding, or in a science test know the explanation for

---

Why did Jason feel so afraid as darkness began to fall?

_____

_____

_____

_____

_____

_____

Figure 5.4 A reading comprehension item

some phenomenon, such as why we experience night and day, those with poor writing skills might not be able to demonstrate their knowledge and understanding in a written response, when they might well have been able to do so if questioned orally.

In the words of Mansell *et al.* (2009: 16), 'A reading test that involves some writing should be designed to reward those who can read well, but who may write badly, rather than those who simply write well'. The same sentiment could be expressed for historical knowledge, geographical knowledge, scientific understanding, and so on. Whenever written responses are demanded in the assessment of knowledge and skills other than the skills of writing then the more extensive the writing required the greater the danger of 'construct clouding'.

This is essentially what construct validity is all about. We usually want an assessment instrument – item, test, questionnaire or observed activity – to focus on one construct or another as 'cleanly' as possible, along with the criteria actually applied in rating pupils' responses or behaviours. Otherwise it will be impossible to interpret the assessment results unambiguously. And if we're not sure what the results are actually telling us about a pupil's state of learning in the target area then any judgement we make of that pupil could be flawed. The validity of the assessment would be in question.

There is another issue raised here as well. Pupils with poor writing skills when faced with a question demanding an open-ended written response, whether in a reading test, a science test, or a test in any other subject, would be very tempted to skip the question altogether, literally providing no evidence at all of the knowledge or skill being assessed. Clearly, where there are high rates of non-response to test items, then, however we choose to define it, the validity both of the items themselves, and in turn of the assessment result for non-responding pupils, must be in doubt.

Content validity, and to some extent construct validity, are generally assessed through a comparison of the knowledge and skill demands of a test item, a practical task or a test against the assessment intention, the 'assessment objective', which in turn reflects teaching–learning objectives. But how pupils' responses are marked or rated – what the assessment criteria look like – also has an impact. Remember that a question becomes a 'test item' only when there is a mark scheme attached. Similarly, a practical task in science or any other subject becomes a 'performance assessment task' only when a suitable rubric is developed for it. Only with both the item, task or test available on the one hand and the marking or rating scheme available on the other can content and construct validity begin to be meaningfully evaluated.

Criterion validity (concurrent validity and predictive validity)

Other forms of validity include concurrent validity and predictive validity. These are both aspects of what has been termed criterion validity. The first aspect, concurrent validity, is about how closely the results of one type of assessment are in line with those of another. If you develop your own reading test for example, then you would be interested to know the extent to which its results align with those of an established commercial test. Would you get the same general results whichever one you used with your pupils? If so then you could have confidence that your own test measures 'reading ability', however defined, as well as the commercial test does, which you will be presuming has been checked professionally for content and construct validity. Expert judgments might alternatively be used to check test or questionnaire results against. These could be your own judgements about where you think your pupils are in reading, or how good they are at collaborating with others, or how much they know about history or science.

Predictive validity, as its name suggests, has to do with how well a set of assessment results can predict assessment outcomes at some future time, in the same or a different subject. An example would be how well Year 6 test results for mathematics can be used to predict pupils' results in this subject in the lower secondary school (to find out, see Strand 2006).

A comment on 'consequential validity'

A great deal has been written over many years about what assessment 'validity' encompasses. In particular, there has been an evolution in thinking that has led to the notion of 'consequential validity' as representing another aspect of some integrated view of validity (Messick 1989). Consequential validity, as the term suggests, focuses on the consequences of assessment. It has to do with the validity of uses of assessment results, rather than with the validity of the assessment instrument or procedure, or with the validity of the assessment results themselves.

For example, suppose that a reading test based exclusively on simple sentence completion items were to be used in some way as an indicator of pupils' 'reading ability'. And suppose that inferences about school or system effectiveness were to be drawn on the basis of the test results. Most educators today would consider that to be a non-valid use of those particular reading test results, given the very narrow way in which 'reading ability' has been defined in the test. For another example, suppose that a questionnaire had been designed to assess pupils' levels of reading enjoyment in Year 6, and the results from that questionnaire were then used to place pupils into sets for English in the lower secondary school. Some would consider this a non-valid use of the questionnaire results, since reading enjoyment in the primary school might not be a good indicator of later performance in the study of literature. But note that any question about 'consequential' validity is directed at the *use made* of the test or questionnaire results. There is not necessarily any doubt about what the test or questionnaire validly measures, or about the validity of the individual test results that the test produces.

The notion of consequential validity has even been applied to formative assessment:

> It is consequential validity which is the basis for validity claims in formative assessment. By definition, the purpose of formative assessment is to lead to further learning. If it fails then, while the intention was formative, the process was not.
>
> Stobart 2006: 136

But however ineffective teachers' assessment feedback to pupils might be, in terms of whether or not the pupils make learning gains as a result, the assessments themselves might be perfectly valid, in terms of content and construct validity. This is an important point to note.

Consequential validity focuses on the validity of uses made of assessment results. But is it appropriate to tar assessment instruments, or the results produced by them, with the label 'non-valid' merely because certain individuals or organisations use those results for what might be non-valid purposes? Some would say yes it is, while others would disagree (e.g. Popham 1997). Certainly it would be difficult for a test developer to anticipate all possible uses that might be made of the test, least of all to guarantee that the test would have consequential validity in all applications (Reckase 1989). Abusive, or ineffective, uses of assessment results for whatever purpose (see Stobart 2008 for an illuminating discussion on this entire issue) do not automatically reduce the validity of the assessment results themselves, as indicators or measures of where pupils are in terms of the abilities and skills the assessment instrument that produced those results was designed to assess. What do you think?

It is important when evaluating assessment validity to distinguish between the validity of the assessment instrument or process, the validity of the outcomes of the assessment (whether scores or classifications), and the validity of subsequent use of the assessment outcomes for whatever purpose.

Take writing as an example. A writing task can pass the validity test as an instrument for producing evidence of a pupil's writing ability, i.e. it can look fine in terms of its content and construct validity, offering pupils a relevant and stimulating topic to write about, such as whether animals should be kept in zoos, or whether more nuclear power plants should be built. But the validity of the actual writing produced by a pupil in response to that task could be in doubt. If the task was carried out in regular class time, after a relevant prior activity or two and a teacher 'contextualisation', that would be a quite different assessment condition than if the test were to be carried out 'cold' in a formal external test, i.e. without any of the usual teacher and peer support. Some would say that the in-class writing would be a more valid representation of a pupil's writing ability than the writing produced 'cold'. Others would disagree, arguing that any support given in the in-class situation would be difficult to control and could therefore 'contaminate' the task performance and in turn the assessment. Where do you stand on this question?

Whichever way the writing assessment is carried out, what then happens to the results of that assessment, how it might be used in school or system evaluation (consequential validity) is a different validity issue.

Crooks *et al.* (1996) usefully sketched an eight-link 'validity chain'. This identified the various stages in an entire assessment process, from administration of the test to end-use of the test results:

- administration
- scoring (item/task marking)
- aggregation (combining item/task scores)
- generalization (to the larger item/task domain)
- extrapolation (to the 'target domain')
- evaluation (of pupil performances, leading to judgements)
- decision (about appropriate action)
- impact (on the individual pupil, school, nation).

At each stage in the process validity can be threatened. For example, under 'administration' threats included low pupil motivation, assessment anxiety, and inappropriate assessment conditions (such as giving pupils more or less time than instructed to complete the test, failing to maintain discipline during the testing so that some pupils would be distracted by others, preventing copying and cheating, and so on). Perhaps you can predict what the threats might be at every other stage?

Validity and the correlation coefficient

Evaluating construct validity, concurrent validity and predictive validity generally requires the analysis of response data, typically involving reporting of correlations.

You will remember that we came across the idea of correlation briefly in the previous chapter, in connection with item discrimination. A correlation coefficient quantifies the strength of a relationship between two variables, and can take values anywhere between +1 and −1. Take height and weight as an example pair of variables. A correlation of +1 would indicate a perfect 'positive' relationship between height and weight, in the sense that as height increased so too would weight, in exact proportion. In other words, both variables would move systematically together, up or down.

Such perfect associations between variables are rare in real life, and certainly height and weight are not perfectly correlated. Think of the people you work with every day or meet on the bus or see in the supermarket. Some people are tall and thin, others are short and stocky, while still others are short and slender. You will not notice any evidence of a *tight* relationship between weight and height. But there *is* a relationship – it is positive but not perfect. If there were no relationship at all between height and weight then the value of the correlation coefficient would be zero, while a coefficient of −1 would indicate the strongest possible negative relationship: as height increases weight decreases in proportion, and vice versa.

Just as you can quantify the strength of association between height and weight, so, too, can you do the same thing for any other pair of variables. These might be test scores on two different tests, for example one test assessing number skills and the other 'measuring and estimating'. Or they might be scores on a test and scores on a questionnaire, reading attainment and reading enjoyment, perhaps. Or they might be the scores of your own pupils on your own 'home-made' reading test and their scores on the commercial standardised test.

Do remember, though, that a strong correlation between two variables simply tells you that the two variables are technically 'associated', and nothing more. The correlation alone gives you no information at all that is useful in helping to interpret the association. So that although a high correlation, for example 0.8, between pupils' results on two different tests can be taken as supportive evidence that the tests measure the same thing, it is not proof of that. Pupils' test scores on mathematics tests and their scores on reading tests are typically quite highly correlated, but no-one would suggest that mathematics and reading tests therefore measure the same thing.

Remember, too, the phrase that you must have heard many times before, that 'correlation is not causation'. Even when we know that two variables are highly correlated we cannot necessarily infer that the relationship is causal. It does not follow from the fact that mathematics and reading test results are typically highly correlated that being good at reading makes you good also at mathematics, or vice versa. Nor could it be sensibly inferred that giving more teaching time to reading and less to mathematics will lead not only to a higher level of reading achievement in your class but also to a higher level of mathematics achievement, or vice versa. No teacher would be tempted to draw such inferences, and seriously think about spending more time teaching reading, which pupils tend to like more than mathematics, on the assumption that the pupils would not only become better readers but would also do better at maths.

But what if the high correlation had been found between reading ability and enjoyment of reading? Would you be tempted this time to think about doing even more than you usually do in the classroom to stimulate an enjoyment of reading in your pupils, on the assumption that this would ensure that they became good readers? In other words, would you automatically assume that pupils who enjoy reading become 'better' readers? You would probably not assume this, even if policy makers sadly often do. As a teacher, you would most likely recognise that the cause and effect relationship, if any exists, could just as likely be the other way around – that the children who are good readers simply tend to enjoy reading and those who are poor readers do not. So that doing everything possible to get your pupils to enjoy reading would not necessarily result in more of them doing any better in reading tests than previous year groups had done. On the other hand, enjoyment of learning can be assumed to increase learning motivation, and no-one would deny that a motivated learner has a better chance of learning and improving knowledge and skills than a pupil without learning motivation!

Assessment reliability

What is 'assessment reliability'?

Assessment reliability has to do with how well we are able to assess what we set out to assess using given tools, and how well we might measure the same thing if our tools or procedures were to be changed in some way. It is essentially to do with 'consistency' in assessment.

If learning could be assessed as easily and as accurately as pupils' heights or weights then 'assessment reliability' would be much less of an issue than it is – or than it should be. But the assessment of learning can be very challenging. The principal reason has to do with the fact that some of the outcomes of learning that we want to assess cannot be directly accessed. Knowledge, abilities, skills and attitudes become visible to us only when demonstrated by pupils in some way, as they answer questions or carry out actions in response to our requests or instructions. Even then, we cannot always be sure that the evidence provided to us in the form of answers or actions is sufficient to infer with confidence anything about the pupil's general state of knowledge, skill or attitude.

If you were to ask pupils for the names and habitats of two minibeasts, for the date the Romans invaded Britain, or for the circuit symbol for a light bulb, then provided they gave you answers you would have some assessment-relevant information for them. You would know that at that particular point in time, under the circumstances in which you posed the questions, the pupils knew or did not know – perhaps knew once but could not now recall – the minibeast facts, the invasion date or the circuit symbol. You do this all the time in your classroom, as you assess your pupils formatively.

But even for such factual knowledge the assessment challenge increases as we attempt to move away from isolated atomistic questions in attempts to measure knowledge, abilities and skills more globally. Knowing the date of the Roman invasion of Britain is one thing, but this alone would tell you little about a pupil's broader state of knowledge, whether of the Roman invasion, or of that whole period of conquest, or of British (or Roman) history in general. Knowing the circuit symbol for a light bulb gives no information about how many other symbols the pupil knows and can correctly match to different circuit components. It also tells you nothing about the pupil's knowledge and understanding of circuitry, or of electricity more generally, theoretical or practical. As the pupil's teacher you would know the broader picture, but an external assessor, a National Curriculum test marker or a school inspector, would not.

Now suppose that we ask pupils to multiply 36 by 5. This new request moves us into even more complex territory. If a pupil provides the right answer to the multiplication question then we would be able to infer two things:

a   that the pupil possesses both the procedural knowledge necessary to perform integer multiplication tasks (for numbers up to two digits), *and*
b   can apply that knowledge skilfully (unless this particular calculation had been memorised, which would be unlikely).

A wrong answer is less easy to interpret. For had the answer been wrong then unless we could directly question the pupil, as you clearly could in your classroom, we would not know whether this resulted from a careless mistake in application, or whether the pupil could not demonstrate the skill of integer multiplication because the underlying procedural knowledge was lacking.

These few examples already demonstrate some of the interesting problems that assessors – teachers and others – face in this particularly challenging area. Knowing some subject-specific facts tells us little about the breadth or depth of a pupil's general knowledge in that subject field. Being able to solve correctly a single multiplication problem tells us nothing about the security of the pupil's multiplication ability, little about other number skills, and nothing at all about other aspects of numeracy or mathematics.

Yet even if we could formally assess every possible fact and every possible skill that is embodied in a subject curriculum we would need to find a way to pull all of the resulting evidence together in some way, if we want to produce summative statements about pupils that might be meaningfully interpreted. It was the requirement that teachers assess large numbers of relatively small aspects of subject performance that proved the greatest difficulty when National Curriculum assessment was first launched in England, Wales and Northern Ireland 20 years ago (Sainsbury 1994; Clarke and Gipps 1998).

If we cannot assess everything, then how do we know how much relevant evidence we need to gather about a pupil for the resulting assessment to be 'dependable' (that is valid and reliable)? Would 20 factual questions about the Roman invasion produce the same assessment outcome for a pupil as 50 questions? What would be the outcome if 10 of the original questions were substituted with 10 different ones?

If any of the questions required an extended written response, would the assessment outcome vary depending on who marked the pupil's response? If the test had been given the day before, or could be given the following week, or in another room, at a different time of day, what difference would that make to the outcome for a pupil? We cannot answer every one of these questions, although we might have our own views about them based on our own experiences with pupils in the classroom. But there are some issues that we *can* explore, for example what differences could arise should different teachers mark the pupil's work.

Reliability has been defined as follows by the Office of Qualifications and Examinations Regulation (Ofqual) in England:

> Reliability refers to the consistency of outcomes that would be observed from an assessment process were it to be repeated. High reliability means that broadly the same outcomes would arise. A range of factors that exist in the assessment process can introduce

unreliability into assessment results. Given the general parameters and controls that have been established for an assessment process – including test specification, administration conditions, approach to marking, linking design and so on – (un)reliability concerns the impact of the particular details that do happen to vary from one assessment to the next for whatever reason.

Quoted in Johnson 2011: 6

Reliability is essentially about precision, consistency, repeatability. Consistency in the outcomes of assessment across different assessment conditions, i.e. repeatability, is essential for assessment reliability.

Sources of 'unreliability'

The principal sources of unreliability in the test-based assessment of learning are the test items or tasks that are used for assessment, and the markers who mark the results.

If a pupil's lengthy written response to a reading comprehension question is marked by person A rather than person B, then there will probably be some difference in the marks awarded for the pupil's response, even after some form of marker training to try to ensure standardisation. This is a principal potential source of assessment unreliability that everyone can understand.

Another major source of variation in test results is the items and tasks themselves. If two or three of the questions in a test were to be replaced with others, would that have an effect on pupils' performances? For some pupils it might do. You will have been assessed yourself at some point in the past. Did you ever come out of the examination room happy that the topics you had revised so well beforehand had 'come up', or dismayed by the fact that they had not? Most of us have experienced this.

When an entire test focuses on a single topic the effect of topic interest on the assessment result can be considerable. Think about a pupil taking the reading test about Jason and his rowing boat presented in Chapter 4. Would the pupil have produced the same quality of performance – shown the same evidence of reading comprehension – if the test had been based on a short story about an alien who fell down a chimney, or a kitten lost in the snow, or a warrior preparing for battle? And what if the source text had been a functional piece, about magnets, perhaps, or Romans, or the Rhine river? What then? Might there be a difference in the performance of the pupil in one or other task, of one or other type? And would boys and girls differ, do you think, in how differently they might react to different reading stimuli?

If you asked a pupil to carry out a science investigation to explore the food preferences of mealworms, would the pupil perform just as well, or just as badly, if you had instead asked him or her to carry out an investigation into friction that involved rolling toy cars down a ramp to compare their speeds?

Another factor that could affect assessment outcomes is the mode of assessment. Would it make any difference to the outcomes if pupils were given the same test to do practically, or interactively on-screen, rather than passively on paper?

Sometimes whole groups of pupils 'interact' differently from others with items of a certain type. If one class had covered fractions more recently than another, for example, then we might expect the pupils in that class to perform better than the others on fraction items. Even if we accept that once taught and mastered such skills are there for life, recent practice could provide an advantage in a testing context. Then again, while all classes might have covered the same material in the same period, perhaps one teacher has been particularly effective in one particular area, and this could show up in better marks in that area for that teacher's pupils. These are just two possible examples of group influences that might lead to inconsistency in pupils' performances on different test items.

We can rarely assume that a test would give the same result for the same child whenever, wherever and however it might be used. Indeed, can we even make that assumption for a single test question, like a minibeasts item? Most class teachers would probably agree that we cannot. Young pupils, like the rest of us, can produce inconsistent performances in a test, or in any other type of assessment activity. This 'interaction' between pupils and test items, this inconsistency in performance, is a potentially important contributor to unreliability in assessment.

Some pupils become flustered with anxiety during formal testing sessions, while others simply refuse to make the effort to show what they can do. Extraneous factors can also have an unpredictable influence, such as distractions inside or outside the classroom. Pupils might be moving around the room, asking for pencils, finishing the test early, or whatever. Dogs might be fighting outside the window, or children chatting loudly in the playground. The heating could have broken in the middle of winter, or a heatwave be raging in June. You will be able to remember numerous other examples of incidents that you were concerned could have affected a pupil's performance in a test. These are all potential contributors to inconsistency in assessment, many of which are beyond our control.

But these are just some of the factors that can affect a pupil's performance on a single task or test. If we consider any test as simply a 'container' for test questions, and any multi-step practical task as a collection of smaller activities, we can imagine that if we replaced some of the questions in that container, or some of the activities in that task, with others then different outcomes could emerge for the same individuals. We need to be aware of this possibility whenever we engage in assessment, and if necessary take action to address it. Then we need some way of determining how good our assessments are, by quantifying their reliability.

To summarise, there are many influences at play in assessment situations that contribute to variation in test scores. These can include:

- the conditions of assessment
  (temperature in the room, distractions inside the room, noise disturbance outside the room, and so on)
- the content of the test or task itself
  (pupils doing better on questions on their favourite topics)
- the composition of the test or task
  (some pupils doing better than others on multiple-choice questions, perhaps)
- marker differences and inconsistency
  (where open-ended questions are involved).

These factors account for some of the observed variation in scores, and this part of the variation is unwanted – it is 'noise' in the assessment process. Technically, we say that factors such as these, and the score variation they create, contribute to 'measurement error' in assessment.

Quantifying score reliability

When we use a single test with a group of pupils the result is a set of scores (marks), one score for every pupil on each question in the test. There will be variation in these scores, some pupils producing high scores for most questions, others low scores for most questions, with typically many in-between, showing a mixed picture. These are scores that we can see. For this reason they are called 'observed scores', and the variation in them is 'observed score variation'. Alongside a pupil's observed score is an idealised quantity called the pupil's 'true score', essentially the score that the pupil could ideally have been expected to achieve, but which we cannot in principle observe directly. The difference between the true score and the observed score is what we call 'measurement error'. Genuine differences among the pupils in terms of what is being assessed – numeracy skills, reading ability, geography knowledge – will normally explain most of the variation in scores. This 'genuine', or 'valid', score variation is technically called 'true score variation'.

Sorting out all the different sources of variation potentially involved in an observed score can become quite a complicated business, and it can often be helpful to use a graphical model to break down the complexity. Figure 5.5 (which is not strictly a Venn diagram, although it looks very similar) identifies the principal contributors to variation in a typical set of item scores. The figure illustrates a situation in which all pupils sit the same test, or set of questions, and all pupil responses to every question are marked independently by two or more markers. Note that questions in a test could equally be replaced in Figure 5.5 by aspects of performance in a complex task rating scheme, such as a marking scheme for writing in which 'spelling', 'grammar', 'audience awareness' and other aspects are rated.

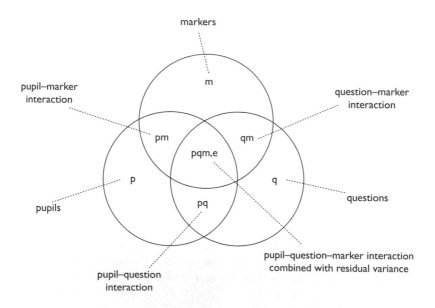

Figure 5.5 Principal contributions to variation in test scores

(Note that the areas in this figure merely identify sources of score variation, their relative sizes convey no information at all about the relative importance of the contributions of those different sources to score variation.)

In the total score variation there will be 'true score' variation, as we have just discussed; this is represented by the area p. There will also be a contribution from differences between the questions (or performance aspects) in terms of their relative difficulty (area q), and from differences between the markers in terms of their overall standards of judgement (area m).

To illustrate a between-pupil difference in scores, Figure 5.6 shows the marks gained on each of 10 test questions by just two different pupils, Jasmine and Chris, in a test in which every question is marked out of three marks (this is a fictitious example, which could be a science test, a geography test, or whatever). Notice that while neither pupil achieves the same mark across all 10 questions, where there are differences in their marks on particular questions it is Jasmine who has the higher mark, the difference usually being one mark. Chris never scores higher than Jasmine. Their average marks on the test as a whole would be 74 per cent and 50 per cent.

In addition we have contributions from what are technically called 'interaction effects', shown as the areas pm ('pupil–marker interaction'), pq ('pupil–question interaction') and qm ('question–marker interaction'). Variation from pupil–marker interaction arises when markers appear to vary in their standards of judgement as they rate different pupils: one marker might give a higher mark to pupil X, or rather to pupil X's piece of writing, than to pupil Y, with another marker doing the opposite. Variation from question–marker interaction occurs when individual markers show inconsistent marking standards from one question to another (or one aspect of writing to another); for example, one marker giving unexpectedly high marks to a particular question or aspect compared with that marker's usual pattern. Variation from pupil–question interaction arises when individual pupils show inconsistent performances on different questions in a test, or across the different performance aspects rated in a writing marking scheme.

Figures 5.6 and 5.7 together illustrate what we mean by 'interaction'. In Figure 5.6 we see that when there are differences in the marks achieved by Jasmine and Chris on the different questions in the test it is Jasmine who always has the higher mark. But Jasmine doesn't get a mark more than Chris on *every* question. This means that there is some evidence of pupil–question interaction going on here. Chris does better than you might expect on a few questions, or equally we could say that Jasmine does worse on some questions than you might expect, given the picture on the majority of questions in the test. Maybe Chris answered a

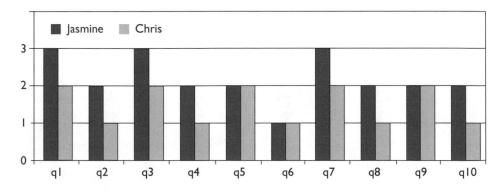

Figure 5.6 Marks scored by Jasmine and Chris on 10 science questions, each question carrying a maximum of three marks

question on food webs, and another on plant labelling, better than the rest, but still not better than Jasmine.

Figure 5.7 illustrates stronger evidence of pupil–question interaction. This chart compares Jasmine's question scores with those of a different pupil, Lee. This time, we not only see 'jagged' profiles for both pupils across the 10 questions, we also see that whereas Jasmine does better than Lee on some questions, Lee, unlike Chris, actually does better than Jasmine on others.

In the intersection of all three circles in Figure 5.5 is the area r that captures all other sources of variation, including declining pupil motivation, classroom disturbances, lapses in concentration, clerical error in mark recording, and so on – all those contributions to score variation that we cannot isolate for separate quantification; this is called 'residual' variation.

Residual variation is a contributor, often an important contributor, to measurement error, whether the assessment is norm-referenced or criterion-referenced (these are explained in Chapter 4). Other error contributors in both types of assessment are the pupil–question and the pupil–marker interactions. This is because the principal aim of such applications is to locate pupils as reliably as possible on the test scale, relative to one another in the case of norm-referenced assessment, and in absolute terms in criterion-referenced assessment. Clearly, if a pupil's test score could vary depending on who marked the test, or who rated the writing, then the pupil's position on the scale could arbitrarily move up or down, both relative to other pupils and absolutely. Similarly, if pupils show uneven performances on the different questions in a test then their location on the test scale could easily shift if different questions were used. The way to counter any such unwanted variation is to increase the number of markers who mark any one script – averaging the result – and to increase the number of questions in the test.

In criterion-referenced applications, there are additional sources of error variation. There is between-marker variation and between-question variation, along with marker–question interaction. This is because when different markers have different overall standards of judgement then if all pupils were marked by both markers you would see that every pupil would have a higher score from one marker than from the other. The *relative* positions of pupils on the score scale would be the same, in other words the rank order would not change. This is why between-marker differences in standards do not contribute to error in norm-referenced

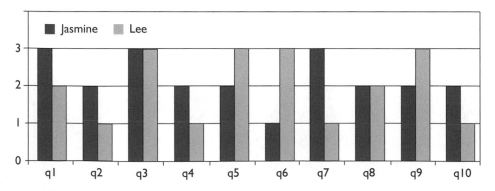

Figure 5.7 Marks scored by Jasmine and Lee on 10 science questions, each question carrying a maximum of three marks

applications. Pupils' *absolute* locations would change, however. This means that if a pre-agreed cut score were to be applied, then whichever marker marked a particular pupil's work could have a very serious impact on the final judgement for that pupil: the pupil could achieve a test score higher than the cut score from one marker but lower than it from another. The way to counter the problem would be to average the marks awarded by two or more markers to any one script (unless marker standardisation could be proved to eliminate any possibility of marker differences in live marking). The same kind of argument applies to the particular set of questions that form the test. The remedy here is to increase as much as practicable the number of questions in the test.

When there is unlikely to be a marker issue, as in an objective test, then markers disappear from the model in Figure 5.5, so that we have only between-question differences in difficulty and inconsistent performances of pupils across questions to worry about. In situations where there is only one 'question', as in a writing test where only one piece of writing is requested and rated holistically, then questions disappear from the model, leaving only markers to contribute in some way to measurement error. Note, though, that having only one piece of writing as evidence of a pupil's writing ability could be misleading. If the pupil had been given a different writing task to do, of a different kind or with a different stimulus topic, then the quality of the writing produced could be different. With just one task there would be no possibility of exploring error contributions from these sources: 'task type' and 'stimulus topic' would be what we call 'hidden factors', factors that might have an impact on assessment reliability but that for one reason or another are beyond investigation.

When constructing tests, we try – or we should try – to construct, administer and mark the test in such a way as to reduce measurement error as much as we can, so that what remains is as close as possible to the 'true score'. To help us quantify how much of the variation in a test score is due to differences in the true scores of the pupils and how much is due to 'error', measurement theorists have constructed a number of 'reliability coefficients', which are computed in different ways, but all of which have analogous interpretation.

Their values all range from 0 to 1 (theoretically, at least). The value of the coefficient tells us how much of the observed score variation is accounted for by 'genuine' between-pupil score variation. For example, if we learn that a reliability coefficient has a value of 0.75 we can read this as indicating that 75 per cent of the variation in pupils' scores is due to real differences in their 'true scores', and the remaining 25 per cent is attributable to errors of measurement, or 'noise'. The theory is that the higher the value of the coefficient the less error, or uncertainty, there is in the test results. In formal testing situations we typically expect to have coefficients above 0.8 (80 per cent of the variance being attributable to valid variance) and preferably above 0.9 (90 per cent valid variance).

The earliest reliability coefficients were calculated simply by correlating pupils' test scores for two administrations of the same test ('test–retest' reliability), for two structurally similar halves of the same test ('split-half' reliability), or for two different 'parallel' forms of a test ('parallel forms' reliability), such as two identically structured numeracy tests. The test–retest approach can lead to problems in interpretation, as you might imagine, when the interval between testing sessions is more than a week or two, or even a day or two. This is partly because learning might have taken place in the meantime, but also because children might remember and discuss test items and so improve their performance on the second occasion. This form is better suited to skills assessment.

Nowadays, the consensus among measurement professionals is to use rather more complicated reliability measures belonging to the class of what are usually called 'internal consistency' indices. These essentially quantify how much consistency there is in pupils' scores across the items within a test. One such index, Kuder-Richardson 21 (or KR21), was originally developed for use with objective tests, and can be applied to any test comprising dichotomously-scored items. A generalised alternative, applicable to any test, however it is marked, is the well-known Cronbach's coefficient alpha, which tends to be used everywhere, by commercial test producers and others, even when it ought not to be (because the assessment is criterion-referenced).

You will find details of all of these different coefficients in any textbook on measurement theory (e.g. Crocker and Algina 2006; Reynolds *et al.* 2008).

Internal consistency measures, including coefficient alpha, are based only on information about the relationship among the items in the test itself, and have nothing to tell us about the relationship between the items in the test and any external criteria. They should therefore only be applied to norm-referenced assessments, even though, regrettably, many assessment practitioners use them, and in particular Cronbach's alpha, indiscriminately in both norm- and criterion-referenced situations. Even for norm-referenced applications these coefficients take just one potential error contributor into account: they cannot, for example, jointly estimate the effect on reliability of both markers and questions simultaneously.

Commercial standardised tests usually report high reliability coefficients, and relatively high coefficients have also been reported for tests used in England's National Curriculum assessment in recent years (Newton 2009). In all these cases the values being quoted are indeed for Cronbach's alpha. Yet despite the fact that many National Curriculum tests – certainly those in reading – include a high proportion of open-ended items, pupil scripts, even for writing itself, are only single-marked. Great attention is paid to the issue of marker standardisation ahead of live marking, and markers are monitored from time to time as they mark, by comparing their judgements on 'seeded scripts' with those of an 'expert marker' ('seeded scripts' are simply scripts pre-marked by the expert marker that are slotted randomly into markers' batches). This cannot, however, prevent differences in markers' standards from occurring and affecting some pupils. With just one marker per script, there is no possibility of calculating a more sophisticated reliability coefficient – a 'generalisability' coefficient – to take contributions to 'measurement error' of markers as well as items into account (Shavelson and Webb 1991 provide an accessible introduction to generalisability theory and generalisability coefficients). So reported reliability estimates in such cases are probably overestimating reality.

Performance investigations, and especially those time-consuming tasks with quite variable content and skill demands, are particularly problematic in terms of both their reliability and their validity. A study in which different students were required to attempt three different science investigation tasks originally designed for exploratory use in Assessment of Performance Unit science surveys in the UK (Harlen 1988) showed that the contribution to measurement error of inconsistent student performance across the tasks was higher than the contribution of markers (Shavelson *et al.* 1992).

As has been noted earlier, the usual way to increase reliability in any test-based assessment is to increase the number of items or tasks involved and/or the number of markers that mark each script. But when the tasks are as 'large' as science investigations it is difficult realistically to contemplate having each pupil undertake more than two or three of them. The consequence is that performance tasks of this type are not easy to use to generate robustly generalisable assessment evidence. Portfolios suffer similar problems.

The special case of teacher assessment

So far this chapter has considered the validity and reliability of test-based assessment. But what about the validity and reliability of teacher assessment, for example when judging pupils' attainment in terms of National Curriculum 'levels'?

It has been noted earlier that all-encompassing timed summative tests inevitably sample the curriculum that they are intended to relate to, and sometimes the sampling can be drastic. The less space there is in a test the fewer are the opportunities to cover more than a handful of aspects of that curriculum, and in consequence the lower will be the test's content validity, even if construct validity is high. It is partly for this reason that there have been pleas for tests to be replaced by teacher judgement, given that teachers are in an unquestionably better position than a test to cover a much larger representation of the curriculum when they assess pupils judgementally, in terms of the number and variety of pieces of knowledge and skill that they can observe and monitor.

Harlen, for example, made the following observation:

> Teachers' judgements can, when moderated, provide more accurate information than external tests because they can cover a much wider range of outcomes and so provide a more complete picture of students' achievements.
>
> Harlen 2007:138

There is little doubt that primary teachers in particular cumulate a wealth of knowledge about their pupils' achievements and capabilities during the long period with which they teach, assess and otherwise interact with them. In principle, therefore, teachers *are* in a better position than a relatively short end-of-period test to provide a valid assessment of those achievements and capabilities. But what do we know *in practice* about how valid teachers' judgements, especially formal level judgements, actually are?

For totally understandable reasons, given the nature of the task, there are many issues surrounding teacher assessment that raise questions about both validity and reliability. One is potential bias, such as consciously or otherwise favouring one pupil over another, or one type of pupil over another (for instance, girls in English for their diligence and tidy work, boys in science for their greater enthusiasm in some areas). Moreover, different teachers might apply different, sometimes personal, assessment criteria when making judgements – how tempting is it to give credit to a child for working hard all through the year, even when that child's achievement in the target subject is only very modest? Moderation exercises are intended to address such issues, so that teachers become aware of possible biases, and can avoid them, and so that they come to a shared understanding about the criteria that they are expected to apply in their assessment practices. But it is very difficult to know how effective any amount of moderation is in this sense, and little if any research has been carried out into how teachers actually do assess their pupils in the classroom.

Some researchers have compared teachers' judgements with test-based level classifications, and have reported mixed results. For a recent example from Scotland, Johnson and Munro (2008) compared the results of both types of assessment in reading, mathematics and science for pupils in four different age-groups (8-, 10-, 12- and 14-year-olds). Both teachers' judgements and test results were in principle criterion-referenced, relating in each subject to the same 5–14 progressive level framework in each subject (for English language see SOED 1991a, for mathematics SOED 1991b and SOEID 1999, and for science Scottish Executive 2000). Teachers adopted a 'best fit' approach using the official level descriptions in the subject frameworks when judging the levels of their pupils. The survey tests were domain-referenced 'single level' tests (unlike the mixed-level tests in England's National Curriculum assessment), with a 'two-thirds correct' cut score used to judge whether a pupil was working at the level of the test or not.

The degree of match between teacher judgements and test results varied from one age group to another and from one subject to another, with science showing the worst outcome. Rates of exact level agreement between teachers and tests were between 45 per cent and 60 per cent for mathematics, depending on pupil age, and at around 40 per cent for reading. In science, however, agreement rates varied between 10 per cent and just under 35 per cent.

National profiles of teachers' level judgements were remarkably similar in all three subjects, judgements tending to 'bunch' around two or three levels, one of which was the 'expected' level for the stage where an expected level existed. In general, for reading and numeracy/mathematics the test results were less favourable than the teachers' judgements for the older stages, but with differences in both directions lower down the primary school. In science, for every age group test-based results were very poor, and markedly less positive than the teachers' judgements. Several possible explanations were offered for this finding, perhaps the most likely being that while the tests were designed to assess 'knowledge and understanding' the teachers were possibly focusing more on investigation skills. If so, then both types of assessment might have been valid, but they were targeting different constructs.

When teachers' level judgements and key stage 2 test results were similarly compared in England, stronger associations emerged (Reeves *et al.* 2001). Exact agreement rates were consistently around 75 per cent in the three years studied in reading, mathematics and science. However, schools had a generous window within which they could submit their teachers' judgements, and this overlapped with their receipt of the test results for their pupils. It is likely, therefore, that in some cases the judgements and the test results were not independent, throwing some doubt on the validity of the agreement rates themselves, and in turn on their interpretation.

As far as the *reliability* of teacher assessment is concerned, very little can be said at this time. Claims have been made that teacher assessment can be highly reliable, perhaps more so than tests. Wiliam, for example, wrote in the context of National Curriculum assessment in England that:

> By using a teacher assessment, we would in effect be using assessments conducted over tens, if not hundreds, of hours for each student, providing a degree of reliability that has never been achieved in any system of timed written examination.
>
> Wiliam 2001: 19

However, even if teachers could in real life find these thousands of hours to devote to assessment, even if only for 'core' subjects, there is no evidence one way or the other about the likely truth of this reliability claim.

It would be difficult, impossible maybe, to evaluate the reliability of an individual teacher's assessment judgement as he or she works interactively with pupils in the classroom itself. What we can do, though, is focus on product evaluation. Where pupils produce a piece of writing, or a portfolio, or a model of some kind, then we have something that we can work with. We can use that resource to explore the degree to which different teachers *do* similarly understand the criteria that should be applied when making evaluative judgements, and *can* arrive at the same view (the same 'attainment level'). Unfortunately, very few empirical studies have been carried out in this area, as recent reviews on the topic of teacher assessment reliability have shown (e.g. Harlen 2004; Johnson 2011).

One example is the Monitoring Children's Progress Project, which ran for three years in England. Its aims included helping teachers to better understand the attainment target criteria in the different National Curriculum core subjects, and to more effectively use Assessing Pupil Progress (APP) materials to confirm their level judgements. The general objective was to facilitate confidence and competence in teacher assessment. The project evaluation confirmed that over the period there was an improvement in teachers' understanding of the assessment criteria, and an improvement in their ability to recognise valid assessment evidence. And towards the end of the experiment, empirical data emerged showing that teachers could reach a reasonably high rate of agreement in their level judgements (see Stanley *et al.* 2009 for an overview of the project and its evaluation).

Writing has frequently featured in attainment surveys in Scotland, and the writing produced by pupils has regularly been rated independently by two or three teacher raters, usually including pupils' own class teachers. The rating process ultimately produces a 'level' for each piece of writing, and percentage agreement rates have routinely been reported. In the 2005 survey, for instance, it was noted that in around a third of cases there was unanimous agreement about the appropriate level for a piece of writing, with the agreement rate rising to 90 per cent for 'majority agreement', i.e. at least two of the three raters independently producing the same level judgement (SSA 2006: 26). In a designed study in 2009, in which level judgements were converted to numeric 'scores', it was established that inconsistency in the judging standards of individual markers as they moved from one piece of writing to another was a more important contributor to score variation than differences between markers in their overall standards of judgement (Johnson 2009).

Questions for reflection

•   Have you ever found yourself having to use a test that you thought had questionable content validity? In what way was it potentially defective?
•   Various different kinds of test have been developed that claim to assess 'reading ability'. Can you name a few? And which of them would you consider offers the most valid reflection of what 'reading ability' is about in your view?
•   Thinking about your own experience in the classroom, what would you say are the biggest threats to the validity of your own assessments of your pupils? Are some subjects more vulnerable in this sense than others? If so, why do you think this is?
•   If you have been involved in moderation recently, what new learning did you come away with as regards the challenges involved in bringing different teachers' assessment criteria and standards of judgement into alignment? Have you ever seen any kind of empirical indicator of the degree of agreement achieved before and after moderation? How effective was the moderation?

Further reading

Crocker, L. and Algina, J. (2006) *Introduction to Classical and Modern Test Theory*, Belmont CA: Wadsworth Group.

Hambleton, R.K., Swaminathan, H. and Rogers, H.J. (1991) *Fundamentals of Item Response Theory*, London: Sage Publications.

Reynolds, C.R., Livingston, R.B. and Willson, V. (2008) *Measurement and Assessment*, Boston: Allyn & Bacon.

Shavelson, R. and Webb, N. (1991) *Generalizability Theory: A Primer,* Newbury Park: CA: Sage.

Statutory assessment

What is the current situation as regards statutory assessment in England's primary schools? At what ages are assessments required, and what form do they take? What are the responsibilities of teachers and their schools in this context? And what is the situation in the other countries of the UK? Chapter 6 answers these questions, describing in some detail the following aspects:

*   Early Years Foundation Stage assessment
*   The proposed phonic screening test in Year 1
*   The National Curriculum and its assessment at key stages 1 and 2
*   The situation in Northern Ireland, Scotland and Wales.

Statutory assessment in England's primary schools

The National Curriculum was introduced into England (and Wales) through the Education Reform Act of 1988, for pupils aged five to sixteen. With it came statutory assessment. While the curriculum and its assessment system have undergone several revisions since inception (see Chapter 7), the most recent in 2011, teachers in England continue to be required to assess pupils in three core subjects – English, mathematics and science – at the end of three 'key stages' in their schooling (Table 6.1). These are key stage 1 and key stage 2 in the primary school, at the end of which pupils are seven or eleven years of age, respectively, and key stage 3 in the lower secondary school, when most pupils are aged 14. At a fourth key stage, key stage 4, most pupils would be taking examinations leading to national qualifications, in particular for the General Certificate of Secondary Education (GCSE). The national qualifications system preceded the launch of the National Curriculum and its assessment system, and the degree to which their different 'syllabuses' might be reconciled has been the subject of some interesting debates – see, for example, Stobart (1991) and Daugherty (1995: chapter 6).

In a more recent development, the youngest age at which children are formally assessed in England has been lowered from age seven to age five, although the five-year-olds in question are unaware that they are being assessed. The Childcare Act of 2006 introduced an Early Years Foundation Stage during which a pre-compulsory education curriculum is offered for children in pre-school centres, nurseries, primary school reception classes, private play groups, and so on. Statutory assessment takes place when children reach the age of five, and is based on practitioners' professional judgement. Meanwhile, the most recent addition to the range of statutory assessments of children in primary schools takes the form of a compulsory phonic test for six-year-olds, a 'phonic check', planned for introduction in 2012.

Table 6.1 The Early Years Foundation Stage and the four National Curriculum key stages

Early years providers*	Early Years Foundation Stage (birth to age 5)
Primary school	Key stage 1: Years 1 and 2 (ages 5–7)
	Key stage 2: Years 3 to 6 (ages 7–11)
Secondary school	Key stage 3: Years 7 to 9 (ages 11–14)
	Key stage 4: Years 10 and 11 (ages 15–16)

Note

* These will include pre-school centres, nursery schools, play groups and primary schools with reception classes

This chapter begins with a look at the assessment requirements in the Early Years Foundation Stage, follows with the phonic check requirement, before overviewing National Curriculum assessment at key stages 1 and 2. The chapter concludes with an overview of the situation in Northern Ireland, Scotland and Wales.

Early Years Foundation Stage assessment

The Early Years Foundation Stage (EYFS) was introduced in 2008. Its curriculum focuses on six 'areas of learning and development':

- personal, social and emotional development
- communication, language and literacy
- problem solving, reasoning and numeracy
- knowledge and understanding of the world
- physical development
- creative development.

These six areas of learning and development were intended to be addressed through 'planned purposeful play', involving a balance between integrated adult-led activities of the kind described in Chapter 2, and child-initiated activities.

EYFS assessment is based on professional judgement, and takes place at the end of the academic year in which the child turns five. Assessment involves completion of an 'EYFS profile' (QCA 2008), through collaboration between early years practitioners, parents and carers. The profile currently includes 13 'assessment scales' across the six areas of learning and development (Table 6.2), embodying 69 learning goals that children are expected to achieve by age five (reduced to 17 in the 2011 review recommendations – more on this below). Each scale includes nine 'scale points' that practitioners must evaluate each child against, giving a total of 117 separate scale point judgements.

The first three scale points are relevant for children who are working towards the early learning goals for that scale; the early learning goals are themselves described in the range of scale points 4 to 8. Scale point 9 describes a child who has met all the early learning goals for that scale and is consistently working beyond them. For example, Table 6.3 shows the scale points for 'dispositions and attitudes' under 'personal, social and emotional development'. For every scale point that the practitioner judges the child to have met the child is (unknowingly) awarded that scale point, giving a possible maximum 'score' of nine scale points for that scale.

Table 6.2 The EYFS 'areas of learning and development', and the 13 separately assessed scales

Personal, social and emotional development	Dispositions and attitudes Social development Emotional development
Communication, language and literacy	Language for communication and thinking Linking sounds and letters Reading Writing
Problem solving, reasoning and numeracy	Numbers as labels and for counting Calculating Shape, space and measures
Knowledge and understanding of the world Physical development Creative development	

Source: QCA 2008: 24

Table 6.3 EYFS scale points for 'dispositions and attitudes'

	Scale point	Assessment criteria
Progressing towards the early learning goals	1	Shows an interest in classroom activities through observation or participation
	2	Dresses, undresses and manages own personal hygiene with adult support
	3	Displays high levels of involvement in self-chosen activities
Early learning goals	4	Dresses and undresses independently and manages own personal hygiene
	5	Selects and uses activities and resources independently
	6	Continues to be interested, motivated and excited to learn
	7	Is confident to try new activities, initiate ideas and speak in a familiar group
	8	Maintains attention and concentrates
Working consistently beyond early learning goals	9	The child has achieved all the early learning goals for dispositions and attitudes. In addition, the child sustains involvement and perseveres, particularly when trying to solve a problem or reach a satisfactory conclusion

Source: QCA 2008: 26–9

When engaging in assessment, practitioners are advised that, 'as a general rule', they should:

- make systematic observations and assessments of each child's achievements, interests and learning styles
- use these observations and assessments to identify learning priorities and plan relevant and motivating learning experiences for each child
- match their observations to expectations of the early learning goals.

QCA 2008: 4

In practice, practitioners will be assessing their pupils continuously, by observing them in integrated activities of the sort described in Chapter 2. But other adults, including parents and carers, are expected to be given the chance to contribute assessment-relevant information for completion of the profile:

> Adults with different roles will have different insights and these must be drawn upon. Assessment must actively engage parents and/or other primary carers, the first educators of children, or it will offer an incomplete picture. Accurate assessment requires a two-way flow of information between setting(s) and home, and reviews of the child's achievements should include those demonstrated at home. Completion of an EYFS profile by the practitioner alone will offer only a partial and incomplete picture of the child's attainment.
>
> QCA 2008: 8–9

As the EYFS profile is intended to be inclusive, early years practitioners are invited to be flexible in the way that they interpret the intentions behind the scale points when assessing children with special educational needs. This would include accepting non-conventional methods of communication, and allowing pupils to use physical aids of various kinds when engaging in activities. Children learning English as an additional language can be assessed in their home language for all aspects of the EYFS profile (all scale points on all scales), with the exception only of some of the scale points under 'communication, language and literacy', which by definition must be assessed in English.

EYFS assessment is intended primarily for the benefit of Year 1 teachers, for use in their child-centred programme planning, and for parents. However, it is also used to help 'evaluate the effectiveness of provision and initiatives' (QCA 2008: 6), and for this reason the profile data are required to be transferred by early years providers to central government. Local authorities are responsible for moderation of EYFS judgements, 'moderation' here being particularly light and informal (see, for example, Cale and Burr 2007).

For a flavour of what the global outcomes of EYFS assessment have looked like, Figure 6.1 illustrates the profile of achievement over the six areas of learning and development in 2010. Within 'personal, social and emotional development', 'personal development' scored higher than 'social development', which scored higher than 'emotional development'. Within 'problem solving, reasoning and numeracy', 'calculation' was the weakest skill area, according to the completed profiles, while in 'communication, language and literacy', writing was the lowest-rated aspect. In every one of the 13 scales girls were more highly rated than boys.

You should note that a government-initiated review of the EYFS in 2010 (the Tickell Review) has led to changes aimed at rationalising the EYFS itself and at simplifying the assessment demands on practitioners (Tickell 2011). The first change is a rationalisation of the 'areas of learning and development', with 'literacy' being separated from 'language and communication', and three 'prime' areas being identified as 'the essential foundations for healthy development, for positive attitudes to relationships and learning, and for progress in key skills such as reading and writing' (Tickell 2011: 20):

- personal, social and emotional development
- communication and language
- physical development.

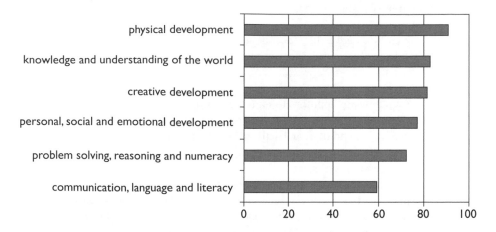

Figure 6.1 EYFS profile results 2010 – the overall picture

(% pupils achieving six or more points within the area of learning; source DfE 2010a: table 3)

Four later areas of learning where the skills acquired in the 'prime' three areas are applied are 'literacy', 'mathematics', 'understanding the world' and 'expressive arts and design'.

The second change is a reduction in the number of early learning goals from 69 to 17, significantly simplifying completion of the new slimmed down EYFS profile. The reduction has apparently been facilitated by the removal of previous goals which were 'not easily observed, ... not sufficiently distinct, and ... not unique to age five as a particular stage of development' (Tickell 2011: 34). However, the previous tick box basis for recording judgements about children's achievement of the learning goals is replaced by a 'best fit' approach involving three descriptive levels of achievement: 'emerging', 'expected' and 'exceeding' (Tickell 2011: annex 5).

Stronger links are also envisaged between the content of the EYFS profile and what is expected of children in key stage 1, to maximise the value of the EYFS assessment for Year 1 teachers and to smooth the transition between EYFS and Year 1 for children.

The proposed phonic screening test in Year 1

In response to government concern at the percentages of pupils in key stages 1 and 2 who have not been reaching their 'target' levels in reading (around 15 per cent of pupils), the latest addition to statutory assessment is a phonic screening test for six-year-olds, known as the 'phonic check' (DfE 2011). Despite the fact that two in every three respondents to the consultation process were against a check focusing on phonic decoding, with the same proportion being against the use of non-words in such a check, the test comprises 40 items, including real words and non-words ('nonsense words'), which each child will be invited by the class teacher to read aloud at the end of Year 1. There will be one version only of the test for use with all the pupils within any one school in any one year, but checks will vary in test content across years. Schools have a one-week window in which to complete the phonic check with all their current Year 1 pupils. A mock test was put through a small-scale pre-trial in 2010 involving 16 schools, followed by a large-scale pilot in a representative sample of around 300 schools in June 2011. Average testing time per pupil is 4–9 minutes (Coldwell *et al.* 2011).

The test has apparently been designed:

> to confirm that children are able to decode using phonics to an appropriate standard by
> the end of Year 1, and to identify those pupils who need additional support.
>
> DfE 2011: 3

It remains to be seen how an 'appropriate standard' for phonic decoding by the end of Year 1 will be decided. However it is defined, it is likely that pupils found not to have reached the expected standard by the end of Year 1 will 'have the opportunity to retake the screening check' in Year 2 (DfE 2011: 6) after receiving appropriate support from their schools to improve their phonic decoding skills.

While the government has confirmed, in response to consultation, that school by school results will not be published, it has nevertheless also confirmed that schools' results, counter to the overwhelmingly negative view of the 1000+ responses to the 2011 consultation, will be required to be submitted centrally for use by other educational professionals 'to drive good quality systematic teaching of phonics in schools' (DfE 2011: 9). National, regional and local authority statistics will be published, even though over 70 per cent of consultation respondents were against this. Pilot study schools were more positive on most issues (Coldwell *et al.* 2011).

The National Curriculum and its assessment

The National Curriculum has been reviewed a number of times since its first launch over 20 years ago, most recently in 2011. As a result there have been some modifications to programmes of study, and the assessment system, too, has been subject to a number of changes over the period: Chapter 7 overviews the evolution. This present chapter looks specifically at *current* statutory assessment requirements for key stages 1 and 2.

The present National Curriculum embodies several individual subject curricula, or 'programmes of study', each broadly defining what has to be taught to pupils in the age range 5 to 16. Three subjects – English, mathematics and science – are designated as 'core' subjects, and it is to these three subjects that statutory assessment currently applies and will probably continue to apply. Other 'foundation' subjects must also be taught but they are not subject to statutory assessment; in 2001 these were art and design, history, geography, information and communication technology (ICT), physical education, design and technology. In addition, schools are required to teach religious education, but pupils are not required to attend classes (parents have the right to withdraw their children) and there is no associated assessment requirement. Since the 1988 Act schools have also been advised to teach personal, social and health education (PSHE) along with citizenship (integrated in the primary school), plus one modern foreign language (from age 11).

The core subject programmes of study as revised in 1999 are given in skeletal outline in Appendix 1. These programmes will be replaced from September 2013 with the outcomes of the latest 2011 revision. It is for individual schools to ensure that during each key stage they cover the relevant programme of study, so that by the end of the key stage their pupils will be as well prepared as possible for assessment against the National Curriculum attainment targets. However, while each programme of study outlines the knowledge, skills and understanding that schools are required to deliver to their pupils, a great deal of flexibility in delivery is given to schools and teachers, both in terms of how they interpret some of the curriculum requirements and in terms of how they plan their teaching programmes over the duration of a key stage. There is no requirement for every school to teach the same part of a programme of study in the same way at the same time.

What is particularly interesting about England's National Curriculum is the fact that while it offers schools a high degree of flexibility in their curriculum planning it very clearly defines when, and to a great extent how, that curriculum should be formally assessed. It identifies 'attainment targets' in each subject, and indicates where the majority of pupils at certain ages are expected to be in terms of their knowledge, skills and abilities. Attainment targets comprise eight progressive 'level descriptions' in each major aspect of a core subject (see Appendix 2 for details), such as 'speaking and listening' in English (see Table 6.4 for levels 1 to 3), 'handling data' in mathematics or 'life processes and living things' in science, plus a description for 'exceptional performance' that would put a child above the highest of the eight levels (relevant only for secondary schools). They were apparently designed so that most pupils would 'progress by approximately one level every two years' (DfE 2010b: 1).

Pupils' progress through the curriculum is expected to be assessed informally by teachers whenever they wish, against the National Curriculum levels or not as they choose. But achievement is *required* to be *formally* assessed in the core subjects at the end of each of key stages 1, 2 and 3. A common set of 'level expectations', or 'standards', applies to all the curriculum subjects (Table 6.5). This indicates the range of levels within which the majority of pupils are expected to be working in each key stage in each subject, and the level most pupils are expected to have attained by the end of the key stage. Whatever the subject, by the end of key stage 1 the majority of seven-year-olds are expected to be able to demonstrate attainment at level 2. By age 11, at the end of key stage 2, the expected level for the majority of pupils is level 4. By the time pupils reach the end of key stage 3, at age 14, most are expected to have attained level 5 or 6.

Table 6.4 Level descriptions 1 to 3 for 'speaking and listening'

Level 1

Pupils talk about matters of immediate interest. They listen to others and usually respond appropriately. They convey simple meanings to a range of listeners, speaking audibly, and begin to extend their ideas or accounts by providing some detail.

Level 2

Pupils begin to show confidence in talking and listening, particularly where the topics interest them. On occasions, they show awareness of the needs of the listener by including relevant detail. In developing and explaining their ideas they speak clearly and use a growing vocabulary. They usually listen carefully and respond with increasing appropriateness to what others say. They are beginning to be aware that in some situations a more formal vocabulary and tone of voice are used.

Level 3

Pupils talk and listen confidently in different contexts, exploring and communicating ideas. In discussion, they show understanding of the main points. Through relevant comments and questions, they show they have listened carefully. They begin to adapt what they say to the needs of the listener, varying the use of vocabulary and the level of detail. They are beginning to be aware of standard English and when it is used.

Source: DfEE/QCA 1999a: 55–6

Table 6.5 Level expectations for each key stage

	Range during key stage	Expected level at the end of the key stage
Key stage 1 (ages 5–7)	1–3	2
Key stage 2 (ages 7–11)	2–5	4
Key stage 3 (ages 11–14)	3–7	5/6

It is likely that Year 2 and Year 6 teachers will be focusing on a small range of levels around the expected level for the stage when attempting to arrive at summative level judgements for their pupils. Thus, for example, when making a level judgement for 'speaking and listening', a Year 2 teacher will probably be evaluating each pupil against the descriptions for levels 1 to 3, shown in Table 6.4, while a Year 6 teacher will probably be checking performance and assessment evidence against the descriptions for levels 3 to 5. From September 2008 teachers have been required to use 'P scales' to assess pupils with special educational needs (SEN) who are working below level 1 in either key stage (consult the government website for details: www.education.gov.uk).

The eight-level framework associated with each subject attainment target is essentially a tool for criterion-referenced assessment. But each level description typically incorporates multiple assessment criteria, which when met contribute to a holistic 'pen portrait' of a pupil supposedly working at that level. In following sections we will consider the inevitable difficulties that teachers face when trying to arrive at level judgements using these complex criterion-referenced frameworks. At the end of key stage 2 teacher assessment is complemented by test-based assessment of pupils' levels, and test developers, too, face challenges when attempting to classify pupils into levels.

From its inception, National Curriculum assessment has had at least three principal purposes:

- To provide information about the attainment of individual pupils, for the benefit of the pupils themselves, their teachers and their parents/carers.
- To produce aggregated pupil attainment data for use in school self-evaluation and external school accountability ('league tables' becoming the most visible sign of this).
- To provide pupil-level attainment results for use in system monitoring.

To serve these purposes the resulting assessment data are made available to parents (for their own children), other teachers in the school, including the headteacher, local authorities and central government. In accountability applications, where both forms of assessment are in operation, the test-based results predominate over teacher judgements.

Teacher assessment at the end of key stage 1

Statutory assessment at the end of key stage 1 is exclusively based on teachers' summative assessments, for English, mathematics and science (QCDA 2010a). The assessment outcomes, the teachers' level judgements, are intended to be based on learners' performances in class throughout the year in a range of different contexts, as noted in the 'breadth of study' section in each programme of study.

In deciding on a pupil's level of attainment teachers are advised 'to judge which description best fits the pupil's performance ... each description should be considered alongside descriptions for adjacent levels' (see, for example, DfEE/QCA 1999a: 54). In other words, as noted earlier, level classification by teacher judgement is in principle an application of criterion-referenced assessment, in which the assessment criteria are embodied in the level descriptions. Each set of level descriptions is in fact a 'best fit' rating scheme for the attainment target in question (but see Sizmur and Sainsbury 1997, and Sainsbury and Sizmur 1998, for interesting discussions on how well the level descriptions actually serve as assessment criteria).

Let us use English for an idea of what is involved in using the sets of level descriptions as 'best fit' schemes. You will remember that there are three attainment targets for English:

1   speaking and listening
2   reading
3   writing.

Teachers are required to produce level judgements for each of these at the end of key stage 1.

Given that the official 'expected level' for the majority of pupils at the end of key stage 1 is level 2, it is unlikely that Year 2 teachers would be expecting many, if any, of their pupils to be working at or above level 4. So they will most probably be using the descriptions for levels 1 to 3 when making their judgements. These are shown for speaking and listening in Table 6.4.

The best fit schemes represented by the sets of progressive level descriptions share some of the characteristics of best fit schemes in general. This is that while the level descriptions give the impression of coherence on first reading, and do seem to reflect learning progression, the descriptions are actually expressed for the most part in quite general terms and they are multifaceted. This is inevitable to some extent, given that each level being described is acknowledged to be 'a broad band of attainment' which 'may be achieved in a variety of ways, taking account of pupils' strengths and weaknesses' (DfEE/QCA 1999a: 7). The level descriptions are holistic pen portraits of pupils at the different levels, as perceived by those subject specialists and policy makers who were involved in development of the various level frameworks.

Because the levels are broad and multifaceted each level description actually embodies a series of specific assessment criteria. Look, for instance, at the description for level 1 in speaking and listening (Table 6.4), which for ease of reference is reproduced again below:

> Pupils talk about matters of immediate interest. They listen to others and usually respond appropriately. They convey simple meanings to a range of listeners, speaking audibly, and begin to extend their ideas or accounts by providing some detail.

When arriving at a judgement about whether a pupil has attained level 1 or not, the teacher must evaluate all of the cumulated knowledge and assessment evidence for that child in terms of four (or five?) different assessment criteria. These are that the pupil:

•   talks about matters of immediate interest
•   listens to others and usually responds appropriately
•   conveys simple meanings to a range of listeners, speaking audibly
•   begins to extend own ideas or accounts by providing some detail.

How would the teacher interpret each of these assessment criteria? For example, look at 'talks about matters of immediate interest'. Don't we all talk about matters of imme- diate interest? Why does this help to define level 1? Is it that level 1 pupils don't talk about anything else, so that if a pupil does occasionally talk about something of less immediate interest that pupil must be level 2 or higher?

Then what about the next criterion: 'listens to others and usually responds appropriately'. Do pupils have to 'listen to others' *and* 'usually respond appropriately' to be considered to have attained level 1? What happens if they simply listen but don't respond? Would that be evidence that the pupil is not working at level 1? That word 'usually' is interesting here as well. How does a teacher decide what 'usually' means in practice? Is it 90 per cent of the time, 75 per cent of the time, half the time? What do you think? And how many times would the teacher have to have observed a pupil interacting with others to be able to judge with confidence whether an 'appropriate response' was *usually* given? We could analyse each statement under level 1, and other levels, in this and other attainment targets, in this and other subjects, in the same way, and wonder how a teacher is expected to interpret the intentions behind the words in terms of identifying and applying appropriate assessment criteria.

The next challenge arises when the different criteria have to be considered as a package. For suppose that a pupil was considered by the teacher to have satisfied one or two of the criteria but not all. The pupil might have no problems talking but could have real difficulty listening to others. How would the teacher weigh up the relative importance of the different criteria in order to arrive at a global judgement? Would satisfying three out of four criteria be enough to confirm a level, no matter which three criteria these were? Faced with a possible dilemma, would the teacher feel the need to look at the level below, if there was one, and to judge the pupil against the criteria for that level? What happens if the same situation arises there as well?

The judgements that teachers are *required* to make of pupils are not easy ones to make. Relatively loose verbal descriptions are always open to an important degree of subjectivity in interpretation, and different class teachers could be forgiven for interpreting them differ- ently, sometimes so differently that the judgements they make might be reflecting different standards of expectation. This is why exemplification is so important in this context, and why within-school and between-school moderation exercises have a vital role to play in helping to pull standards together, if indeed standards of judgements *can* be brought exactly into line.

To support teachers when making level judgement, tasks and tests are made available for them to use in the classroom in English (reading and writing) and mathematics. Teachers are expected to use some of these, but not necessarily all of them, during the key stage. In addition, there are optional tasks 'for children who have followed a curriculum that blends a faster pace, more breadth and greater depth' (QCDA 2010a: 10), i.e. for children who have completed the key stage 1 programme of study and are ready to move on to the programme of study for key stage 2. Task and test results are not gathered centrally.

Moderation

Local authorities are responsible for organising moderation for key stage 1 assessment, although, like the EYFS, this is closer to ratification (principally establishing that assess- ment procedures are adhered to) than genuine moderation (evaluating the appropriateness of teachers' level judgements). Moderators periodically make half-day visits to schools, and talk with the headteacher and class teachers, to establish that they are fully conversant with the assessment requirements and diligent in implementing them. They might also speak for a few minutes with a handful of individual pupils, though in doing this they could not be expected to confirm with any great confidence the particular level judgements given by class teachers to every Year 2 pupil in the school. There is no empirical evidence available concerning rates of agreement among teachers when teachers independently decide pupil levels before or after moderation, so we cannot know what degree of reliability in judgement is actually achieved in practice as a result of all the moderation activity.

2010 results

It might be interesting to see the latest global result of key stage 1 assessment, which involved tens of thousands of teachers assessing over half a million seven-year-olds in five different subject areas. Table 6.6 gives the 2010 attainment results, which are closely in line with results for immediately preceding years: 60–70 per cent of pupils were judged at level 2, with 80–90 per cent judged at level 2 or above. Given what you know about the expected level for pupils at the end of key stage 2, you might not be surprised by these results, which confirm that, according to their teachers, most of the pupils had indeed achieved level 2, with many already beyond it.

Another notable feature in Table 6.6 is that reading shows the most positive picture of achievement and writing the worst. But this does not necessarily mean that in absolute terms pupils are best at reading and worst at writing. Even though an eight-level framework has been developed for application across all subjects the assessment criteria within each level description are clearly subject-bound. A level 2 in reading cannot necessarily be meaningfully compared with a level 2 in writing or in science or mathematics, any more than a grade B in GCSE English can meaningfully be compared with a grade B in GCSE history, physics or business studies.

Another feature in the 2010 results, which is again in line with previous years, is the pattern of gender difference across the five subjects/areas. Looking at the 'level 2 or higher' results, Figure 6.2 shows a gender gap in favour of girls throughout, with larger gaps in the English attainment targets than in mathematics and science. Proportionally more boys than girls, however, achieved level 3 or higher in mathematics and science: this is a common pattern in these subjects that has been noted many times in national and international survey programmes.

Table 6.6 National results for key stage 1 teacher assessment in 2010

	Below level 2	Level 2	Above level 2
Speaking and listening	13	66	21
Reading	15	59	26
Writing	19	69	12
Mathematics	11	69	20
Science	11	68	21

Source: DfE 2010b: 2–4

Note
(% pupils judged in each band)

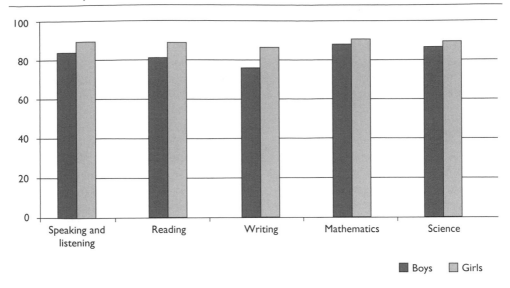

Figure 6.2 National results for key stage 1 teacher assessment in 2010, by gender (% pupils judged at level 2 or higher; source DfE 2010d: table 2)

Teacher assessment at the end of key stage 2

Assessment at the end of key stage 2 differs from that at the end of key stage 1 in the sense that we now have two forms of summative assessment in operation in the three core subjects: teachers' level judgements, as for key stage 1, but also time-constrained test-based assessment. The two forms of assessment are seen as providing complementary information about pupils' attainment:

> The tests are designed to show what pupils have achieved in selected parts of a subject at the end of each Key Stage. Teacher assessment (TA) is the teachers' judgement of pupils' performance in the whole subject over the whole academic year.
>
> DfE 2010d: 9

The outcomes of both forms of assessment for English and mathematics are reported to parents, and collected by local authorities before being forwarded to central government. In science, teacher judgements are reported to parents, local authorities and central government, while the sample-based test results are submitted to central government.

Paralleling the assessment obligations of Year 2 teachers for pupils at the end of key stage 1, Year 6 teachers are similarly required to provide level judgements for each of their pupils in the three core subjects at the end of key stage 2, using the eight-level framework. To support teachers in making their judgements, Assessing Pupil Progress (APP) materials in primary science, English and mathematics are made available to schools.

Teachers are required to make level judgements for each attainment target within each subject, as are their key stage 1 colleagues, and they are expected to combine these to produce overall subject-level judgements using a given calculation algorithm (QCDA 2011a). Basically, the attainment targets within each subject are weighted, equally in English but unequally in mathematics and science, and averaged. The weighted average is then rounded to arrive at an overall level. Where a pupil is judged to be working below level 1 in any attainment target then a zero is allocated to that attainment target for the purpose of averaging.

For example, if a pupil was judged at level 2 for 'speaking and listening', level 3 for 'reading' and level 2 for 'writing', all three being equally weighted, then the level sum is simply 7 and the average is 2.33. The pupil's overall level for English is then judged to be level 2. If a pupil was given level 1 for 'speaking and listening', level 1 for reading and 'below level 1' for writing, the three 'scores' to be averaged would be 1, 1 and 0, giving an average of 0.67, and an overall level 1.

In mathematics the highest weight is given to 'number' (at 5), the lowest to 'handling data' (at 1), with equal weights (2) given to each of 'using and applying mathematics' and 'shape, space and measures'. The four level judgements are multiplied by their respective weights, summed and divided by four to find the average. The average is then as before rounded up or down to produce the integer final level. In science, 'life processes and living things', 'materials and their properties' and 'physical processes' are given an equal weighting, with 'scientific enquiry' given a double weight. Because of the different attainment target weights, the 'overall level' calculations for mathematics and science are slightly more challenging than in English, but the algorithm is exactly the same.

For interest, national results for the school year 2009/10 are shown in Table 6.7. In every subject around half the pupils were judged to be at level 4 with another third or more judged to be working at an even higher level. Just one in five pupils were below level 4 in English and mathematics, with an even smaller proportion in this group for science. The same general distribution has held quite steady over recent years. Would you say these results confirm the official attainment expectations, or do they exceed them? Is the picture one that applies to your own school?

Interestingly, in line with previous years' results, there were slight differences in favour of girls in science (86 per cent of girls versus 84 per cent of boys judged at level 4 or higher) and in mathematics (82 per cent versus 81 per cent), and a quite large difference in their favour in English (86 per cent versus 76 per cent), as Figure 6.3 illustrates.

The teachers' judgements for individual pupils are made available to the children's parents, naturally, and also to the school's headteacher, for school self-evaluation purposes. They are also submitted by the school to the local authority and from there to central government, with a two-month submission window stretching from early May to early July. While in principle teachers' summative judgements complement the test-based results at key stage 2, they have always in practice been considered subsidiary to these. It is the test-based results that form

Table 6.7 National results for key stage 2 teacher assessment in 2010

	Below level 4*	Level 4	Above level 4
English	19	49	32
Mathematics	19	46	35
Science	15	48	37

Note
* Includes absent pupils
(% pupils judged in each band)

Source: DfE 2010d: 5

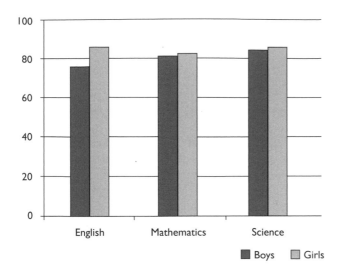

Figure 6.3 National results for key stage 2 teacher assessment in 2010, by gender

(% pupils judged at level 4 or higher; source DfE 2010d)

the basis for school league tables and for over-time system monitoring. System evaluation is discussed in Chapter 7.

Test-based assessment at the end of key stage 2

Key stage 2 tests change from one year to another, but within any particular year every Year 6 pupil takes exactly the same tests in each core subject. Tests are professionally developed by test development agencies commissioned by the government. They are attractive in appearance and imaginative in their item content, and therefore probably motivating for pupils. The tests are formally pretested more than a year before live use, and are taken by pupils under very strict controls designed to standardise the conditions of assessment (see, for example, QCDA 2011b). Completed tests are externally marked.

Each test, or set of tests, is intended to be capable of classifying pupils into one or other of levels 3 to 5 on the basis of their total scores. In 2010 pupils in just over 200 schools took 'single level' tests in mathematics in place of the regular key stage 2 tests, and were awarded their National Curriculum levels on this basis (single level tests in reading, writing and mathematics were piloted and evaluated in the late 2000s, but have not been adopted for roll-out; for the full evaluation see DfE 2010c).

An important change in the general pattern of test-based assessment in science at this key stage is that in 2010 the blanket testing of Year 6 pupils in this subject, i.e. cohort testing, was replaced by a sample-based attainment survey. So that while every Year 6 pupil continues to be formally tested in English and mathematics not every pupil is now formally tested in science. Each year a nationally representative sample of primary schools is randomly selected for participation in the science testing, and within these schools all 'eligible' pupils are tested, where 'eligible' means that the headteacher (clearly in practice the pupil's class teacher) considers the pupil to be at level 3 or higher (QCDA 2010b gives details of the sampling methodology).

The general aim of the new sample-based testing is to *estimate* the overall proportion of pupils in England who attain level 4 or above in science each year, the results being published at the beginning of the autumn term. Schools, and their local authorities, are informed in February if they have been randomly selected to participate in the science testing that year, and at that time they also receive details of the arrangements for administering the tests (see QCDA 2010c for an overview of the assessment arrangements in 2010). Participation is statutory, and testing takes place in May.

A consequence of the change in the pattern of key stage 2 science test-based assessment is that between-school comparisons are no longer possible for this subject on the basis of test results (other than for the participating schools in any year should the current policy of not offering between-school comparisons for science be changed at some point). This means that national and authority school league tables can no longer be produced. Many would say this is a good outcome, others would disagree. Where do you stand on this question?

Test-based assessment in English

Formal testing in English has taken the same general form for the past several years. But only two of the three attainment targets in English are assessed. These are reading and writing. There are no National Curriculum tests for 'speaking and listening': this has been identified as a major threat to the construct validity of 'English' as reported on the basis of test results (Stobart 2009).

Reading is assessed using a timed 45-minute test. Even if you have not seen a National Curriculum reading test, the test format will not surprise you: it comprises a text, or a set of shorter texts, followed by a series of test questions (items). Pupils have 15 minutes to read the text(s) before starting on the test itself. A number of 'assessment focuses', or aspects of reading, shape the questioning. In principle, the aim of the testing is to assess each pupil's ability to:

1   use a range of strategies, including accurate decoding of text, to read for meaning
2   understand, describe, select or retrieve information, events or ideas from texts and use quotation and reference to text
3   deduce, infer or interpret information, events or ideas from texts
4   identify and comment on the structure and organisation of texts, including grammatical and presentational features at text level
5   explain and comment on writers' use of language, including grammatical and literary features at word and sentence level
6   identify and comment on writers' purposes and viewpoints, and the overall effect of the text on the reader
7   relate texts to their social, cultural and historical contexts and literary traditions.

Twist and Sainsbury 2009: 287

From what you have read in Chapter 4, you will realise instantly that a single 45-minute test would have difficulty covering all of the 'assessment focuses' evenly. Test questions are based on the source text(s), and any reading test developer will tell you that different texts lend themselves to differing extents to different mixes of assessment focus. So every year the one test that all Year 6 pupils take will inevitably represent a sample of the seven assessment focuses, quite likely with an uneven coverage.

A reading test typically contains a variety of different question types, of the sort illustrated in Chapter 3. These include short-answer in one or more forms, mainly requiring the pupil to locate and retrieve atomistic pieces of information from the text, aided summary completion, and extended response items that usually demand an explanation or interpretation of some aspect of the text. Short-answer items typically merit one mark each with extended response items meriting up to two marks each. The total mark allocation is 50.

Writing assessment is currently based on two writing tasks, one short and one long, and a spelling test. The marking scheme for the 20-minute short task covers 'sentence structure, punctuation and text organisation' (for four marks) and 'composition and effect' (for eight marks). The marking scheme for the 45-minute long task covers 'sentence structures and punctuation' (eight marks), 'test structure and organisation' (eight marks), 'composition and effect' (12 marks) and handwriting (three marks); pupils are given 10 minutes' planning time before starting to write. In future teacher assessment will replace the composition tasks (Bew 2011).

The strictly timed spelling test is paced by an audio recording (in the case of technical problems the supervising teacher reads out the transcript). The recorded text could be a short story or extract from a longer text, and in appearance resembles a summary completion exercise. The pupil has a paper copy of the recorded text, with 20 gaps indicating 20 missing words. The pupil is to fill the gaps by writing out the words as they hear them. For every three words correctly spelled, up to 18, the pupil gains one mark, with a final mark for 19 or 20 correctly spelled words, for a possible total of seven marks.

Together the writing tasks and spelling test carry a maximum of 50 marks, matching the 50-mark total for reading, for a 100-mark maximum for English (that is for English without 'speaking and listening').

Test-based assessment in mathematics

Test-based mathematics assessment currently relies on two 45-minute tests for 40 marks each, one to be done without the aid of a calculator, and a mental mathematics test for 20 marks. The format of the two pencil-and-paper tests is very similar, each comprising a series of 20–25 'atomistic' test items. The items are for the most part constructed response, mainly short-answer, and sometimes involving drawing (e.g. lines of symmetry, shapes), with a few multiple-choice items also here and there. The mental mathematics test comprises 20 atomistic items, mainly short-answer but with one or two multiple-choice items among them (for example, pupils might be asked to identify the triangle shown among different shapes on a card, or to identify the smallest number in a set of choices). For the most part the items cover the four operations, including applications involving time and money, and fractions.

Between them the tests sample the mathematics curriculum for key stage 2. Note, though, that there is no test-based assessment of 'using and applying mathematics', which for validity reasons would demand an appeal to practical activities of various sorts, including problem solving tasks, discussions, and so on.

Test-based assessment in science

Test-based science assessment is based on two 45-minute pencil-and-paper tests, each with a maximum allocation of 40 marks. The format of the two tests is similar – each consists of a number of structured questions, with items within questions linked to a common theme, such as 'pond dipping', 'building materials', 'at the swimming pool', and so on. The items within and across the structured questions are many and varied, including multiple-choice, short-answer, true–false, sequencing and extended response, tapping a variety of knowledge, skills and understanding.

Between them the two tests sample the key stage 2 curriculum for science. But they do not address the necessarily practically-focused application of knowledge, skill and understanding that is the attainment target 'scientific enquiry'. This means that, as in English and mathematics, one important aspect of subject learning is missing from the test-based assessment of science.

Test results in 2010

The National Curriculum tests do not focus on any particular level. If they did, then pupils' performances on them would in principle be directly comparable to the criterion-referenced assessment that teachers are required to make of their pupils. Because they do not relate to a single level, but span levels, some way had to be found to convert test scores to levels for pupil classification. For this purpose threshold marks are identified each year using the complex process involving statisticians and subject specialists briefly outlined in Chapter 4 (see also QCA 2007 for a relatively accessible explanation). Table 6.8 records the overall results of the 'levelling' procedure in 2010, for the cohort in English and mathematics (DfE 2010d) and for a pupil sample in science (DfE 2010e): note the similarity to the teachers' judgement results given in Table 6.7.

There was no gender difference in mathematics or science (79 per cent of both groups achieving level 4 or higher in mathematics; 80 per cent for boys and 81 per cent for girls in science, not a significant difference either statistically or educationally speaking). In English, following a well-established pattern, girls produced markedly better performances than boys (85 per cent and 75 per cent, respectively, achieving level 4 or higher).

Assessment validity and reliability

The tests that have been used in National Curriculum assessment in the three core subjects would probably be considered by most people as attractive and relevant for 11-year-olds, as well as being valid in terms of their content, and possibly also construct, validity (without access to the relevant empirical data this is impossible to judge). The reliability of the test scores that the tests produce has also been established as acceptable (Newton 2009, using Cronbach's coefficient alpha), although the effect of markers on reliability has not been open to investigation, given that each pupil script is marked by just one single marker (note,

Table 6.8 National results for key stage 2 test-based assessment in 2010

	Below level 4	Level 4	Above level 4
English	20	47	33
Mathematics	21	45	34
Science*	19	53	28

Notes
* Sample-based estimates
(% pupils judged in each band)

Sources: DfE 2010d and 2010e

though, that marker reliability studies have been carried out recently that could lead to a change in practice (QCA 2009). In writing, the achievements of different pupils are potentially affected by the stimulus topic used in any particular year. But because just one topic is used each time for the 'long' writing, there is no useful means of exploring the effect of topic on the reliability of writing assessment.

The validity of the attainment results produced when the test results in the different attainment targets are combined has been the subject of doubt. The objects of the criticism have already been identified above: the absence in the combined assessments of 'speaking and listening' in English, 'using and applying' in mathematics, and 'scientific enquiry' in science. No evidence is available about the reliability of the composite scores.

Interestingly, an aspect that has not been unduly questioned is the use of one single test each year in reading, or one single pair of tests in science and mathematics. The scope for curriculum coverage offered by this strategy is extremely limited. As a result the attainment information being produced in all of the assessment activity is in many senses impoverished.

The situation in Northern Ireland, Scotland and Wales

Wales

When the National Curriculum for England was launched in the late 1980s it was simultaneously adopted for Wales, as was the attendant statutory assessment system. However, the curriculum and assessment system in Wales has since 'evolved from common foundations into a system that is now distinct from that of England' (Daugherty 2009: 247).

Already in 1988 a decision had been made to include Welsh in place of English as one of the core subjects for pupils being educated in Welsh-medium schools. For the other two core subjects, mathematics and science, tests would be made available in both languages for pupils in Welsh-medium or bilingual schools. Also, unlike the situation in England, National Curriculum assessment in Wales included the test-based assessment of speaking and listening as well as reading and writing.

A curriculum revision was eventually implemented in Wales soon after devolution saw the establishment of the Welsh Assembly Government. This broadly resembled the revised curriculum adopted in England in 1999, though with Welsh continuing to feature as a core subject for children in Welsh-speaking schools. Statutory assessment, too, followed the English pattern in general terms. But testing at the end of key stage 1 was dropped in Wales in 2002, and from 2005, acting on an Assessment Review commissioned by the Welsh Assembly (Daugherty 2004), Wales also abandoned test-based assessment at key stages 2 and 3. The country now relies uniquely on teacher assessment at the end of key stages 1, 2 and 3 for all reporting and evaluation purposes, including system monitoring. Teachers are encouraged to apply formative assessment principles in their teaching and assessment practice, and optional tasks are available to them to help with summative assessment (see Cox 2008 for information about the development of optional materials for English).

In the latest development, a play-based 'Foundation Phase' for 3- to 7-year-olds has just been introduced in Wales, which subsumes key stage 1 (a four-year implementation period ended with Year 2 in 2011/12). The old level-based assessment of core National Curriculum subjects at the end of key stage 1 is now replaced with grade-based assessment of 'outcomes' at the end of the foundation phase.

The level-based assessment of core subjects at the end of key stage 1 focused on English or Welsh (depending which language medium the child was being educated in), mathematics and science. As in England, teachers were required wherever possible to provide a level judgement for each pupil for each core subject attainment target, and an overall weighted level for the subject as a whole (DCELLS 2009a). For English, the three attainment targets – oracy, reading and writing – carried equal weight, while for Welsh oracy carried twice the weight of reading and writing. For mathematics 'number' had double the weight of each of the other two attainment targets, namely 'using and applying mathematics' and 'shape, space and measures'. In science, 'scientific enquiry' had zero weight, the other three attainment targets – 'life processes and living things', 'materials and their properties' and 'physical processes' – having equal weights.

The new Foundation Phase curriculum focuses on seven 'areas of learning' (DCELLS 2008a). These share many similarities with England's EYFS 'areas of learning and development', but there are also differences, in particular the higher emphasis given to well-being:

- personal and social development, well-being and cultural diversity
- language, literacy and communication
- mathematical development
- Welsh language development
- knowledge and understanding of the world
- physical development
- creative development.

For each area of learning an educational programme sets out what children should be taught, and six associated 'outcomes' set out the expected standards of children's performance (DCELLS 2008a): the first three outcomes have been designed to be approximately equivalent to levels 1 to 3 in the National Curriculum. At the end of the Foundation Phase, Year 2 teachers are required to arrive at 'outcome grade' judgements for their pupils for the first three areas of learning in the list (DCELLS 2009b).

National Curriculum assessment continues at key stage 2, though with reference to a revised curriculum, 'Curriculum 2008', that was phased into key stage 2 in the years 2008/09 and 2009/10. The core subjects are English, Welsh first language (if the pupil is following the Welsh Programme of Study) or Welsh second language (this became a statutory requirement in 2009/10), mathematics and science. For current programmes of study and level descriptions see DCELLS 2008b for English, 2008c for Welsh, 2008d for mathematics, and 2008e for science. When calculating a weighted average level for English the three attainment targets carry equal weight (DCELLS 2009a). In Welsh, on the other hand, the relative weight given to oracy, reading and writing differ markedly between Welsh first language (4, 3, 3) and Welsh second language (7, 1.5, 1.5).

Since September 2007 schools have been expected to engage in school-based standardisation and moderation at key stages 2 and 3, while from September 2008 teachers have been engaged in cluster-group moderation of examples of their pupils' work to develop a shared understanding of national standards (DCELLS 2008f). An external moderation pilot study was organised in 2010 by the Welsh Joint Education Committee on behalf of the Department for Children, Education, Lifelong Learning and Skills (for details see WJEC 2010). The next phase is moderation roll-out.

At the time of writing, no empirical evidence was available about the degree to which moderation can achieve high rates of agreement among teachers when they work independently (Estyn 2010). This means that the validity and reliability of teacher assessment in this country, as in England, have yet to be formally investigated. Until these issues *are* investigated, we cannot judge the likely wisdom of a total reliance on teachers' judgements for accountability purposes, including over-time system evaluation.

Northern Ireland

Until 2007 the school curriculum in Northern Ireland was a 'local version' of the National Curriculum in England. It was adapted to reflect 'aspects of the difference and diversity in community life' (Elwood 2009: 251), with the programmes of study for history and religious education the most locally contextualised. Otherwise the pattern that pertained in England applied here, too. Assessment of the same three core subjects – English, mathematics and science – took place at the end of the same three key stages as in England. However, while assessment at age seven was based uniquely on teacher judgement, as in England, assessment at the end of key stage 2 was also mainly teacher judgement. There were no tests for 11-year-olds, as there are in England. This is principally because Northern Ireland still had in place the '11+' examination for selection into grammar schools, an examination that was explicitly based on aspects of the key stage 2 curriculum in the core subjects: current arrangements for transfer to post-primary schooling are non-statutory and are carried out by test providers at the request of consortia of grammar schools (Elwood 2011, personal communication). Test-based assessment was practised at the end of key stage 3, as in England pre-2009.

A new revised curriculum and assessment system was launched in Northern Ireland in 2007, and was progressively implemented over a period of three years. This brought in a reduced curriculum content, a focus on skills, and the elimination of testing at the end of key stage 3. Thus for all three key stages spanning primary and early secondary education, National Curriculum assessment in Northern Ireland, as in Wales, now relies exclusively on teacher judgement.

Each pupil in each year of key stage 2 must be assessed in the autumn term for literacy (reading) and numeracy, using a designated computer-based system ('computer-adaptive assessment' – see Chapter 4 for a definition of this); pupils in other years may also be assessed, but assessment for them is not statutory (interestingly, in the 2007 Order (DENI 2007) concerning assessment arrangements this computer-based assessment was intended to be statutory for the second year of key stage 1 as well as all years of key stage 2). The primary purpose of this assessment is 'to contribute to diagnostic support for pupils' learning' (DENI 2010: 3). School results are fed back only to the schools concerned. For their part schools are required to provide parents with the reading and mathematics results of their own pupils.

Each pupil in every year in key stages 1, 2 and 3 *must* be assessed by a teacher at the end of the summer term in each of a number of 'areas of learning', each of a number of cross-curricular skills and 'other skills'. The 'areas of learning' at the foundation stage and key stages 1 and 2 are:

- language and literacy
- mathematics and numeracy
- the arts
- the world around us
- personal development and mutual understanding
- physical development and movement.

while the 'other skills' are:

- thinking, problem solving and decision making
- self management
- working with others
- managing information
- being creative.

Assessment of the cross-curricular skills – 'communication', 'using mathematics' and 'using ICT' – with reference to 'levels of progression' is in the process of introduction (2012/13 school year for 'communication' and 'using mathematics', and 2013/14 for 'using ICT').

Paralleling the situation in England and Wales, there are no empirical indicators currently available about the degree to which teachers' assessments of their pupils are in agreement when made independently. In other words, there is no evidence one way or the other about the validity or the reliability of teacher assessment for any of the elements of pupil learning that teachers in this country are required to assess.

Scotland

There has never been statutory assessment in Scotland. However, the voluntary submission of teachers' assessments of pupils' level attainments with respect to the now defunct 5–14 National Curriculum became almost universal through the 1990s and early 2000s. This was partly through pressure on schools from local education authorities for accountability purposes. The teachers' level judgements were available to parents and to other teachers in the schools, and were used by local authorities and the school inspectorate for school comparisons, i.e. for school evaluation. They were also in part used by the government for system monitoring (though not officially), as was achievement in Scottish qualifications and the results of dedicated sample-based attainment survey programmes (Chapter 7 offers more information about this). The well-established 5–14 curriculum has recently been replaced by the 'Curriculum for Excellence' (Scottish Government 2010a). At the time of writing it is not entirely clear how teachers will be expected to report their pupils' attainment with respect to this curriculum, but assessment will not be statutory.

Questions for reflection

- There is disagreement among teachers about the acceptability of using non-words in a phonic decoding test. But using real words alone could be problematic for different reasons. What do you think are the merits and drawbacks of testing pupils' decoding skills with real or non-real words?
- In National Curriculum assessment in England class teachers are expected to provide 'level' judgements for each of their pupils in each separate aspect of each core subject. If you have been required to do this, what do you see as the particular challenges involved? If you have not been involved in this activity can you instead imagine what the challenges might be?
- If you have been involved in moderation exercises, within your own school, within a school cluster or in a larger context, how do you think this has benefited your ability to 'level' your pupils validly and reliably? If such exercises have ever attempted to quantify the degree of agreement between different teachers when rating the same pupils, was the result what you would have expected? Explain.

- How much do you know about how pupils are assigned to levels on the basis of their National Curriculum test scores? How valid do you think level classifications made using quite unfocused tests can be? What are the issues?

Further reading

Alexander, R. (ed) (2009) *Children, their World, their Education,* Final Report and Recommendations of the Primary Curriculum Review, London: Routledge.

DfEE/QCA (1999a) *The National Curriculum for England: English Key Stages 1–4*, London: Department for Education and Employment and Qualifications and Curriculum Authority. Available online at https://www.education.gov.uk/publications/eOrderingDownload/QCA-99-459.pdf, accessed 25 May 2011.

DfEE/QCA (1999b) *The National Curriculum for England: Mathematics Key Stages 1–4*, London: Department for Education and Employment and Qualifications and Curriculum Authority. Available online at https://www.education.gov.uk/publications/eOrderingDownload/QCA-99-460.pdf, accessed 25 May 2011.

DfEE/QCA (1999c) *The National Curriculum for England: Science Key Stages 1–4*, London: Department for Education and Employment and Qualifications and Curriculum Authority. Available online at https://www.education.gov.uk/publications/eOrderingDownload/DfES-0303-2004.pdf, accessed 25 May 2011.

Tickell, C. (2011) *The Early Years: Foundations for Life, Health and Learning*, An Independent Report on the Early Years Foundation Stage to Her Majesty's Government. Available online at http://media.education.gov.uk/MediaFiles/B/1/5/%7BB15EFF0D-A4DF-4294-93A1-1E1B88C13F68%7DTickell%20review.pdf, accessed 25 May 2011.

System evaluation

What is system evaluation? Why are governments around the world engaged in this activity? What forms can system evaluation take? Is England's National Curriculum assessment a system evaluation tool? What have we learned from system evaluation thus far? What do TIMSS, PIRLS and PISA stand for, and why should they interest primary teachers in the UK? Chapter 7 focuses on such questions, looking specifically at:

- England's system monitoring history
- the situation in Northern Ireland, Scotland and Wales
- international comparative surveys: TIMSS and PIRLS
- the OECD PISA programme.

What is system evaluation?

Governments have a natural interest in knowing how well their educational systems are working. More than this, they have a clear responsibility for evaluating how effective their educational provision is in terms of student outcomes, including academic achievement. Strengths are important to identify, so that they might be built on in the future to further improve effectiveness. And when systems are found wanting policy makers need as much information as possible about where the weaknesses are, so that they can seek ways to address them.

Policy makers, and politicians, use assessment results in their system evaluation in a number of ways. These include comparing:

- cohort attainment with 'national targets' (e.g. the proportion of Year 6 pupils attaining level 4)
- schools with one another, to judge relative 'effectiveness' ('league tables')
- pupil subgroups with one another (e.g. boys and girls), to monitor policy initiatives
- their own system with others, for an international contextualisation
- any or all of the above over time ('system monitoring').

The UK – more specifically England and Scotland – has a long history of system evaluation and monitoring that stretches back several decades. The launch of some important international survey programmes has hugely expanded the information base available to support this activity. Two of the international programmes assess pupils in the primary school (Year 5 in England, P5 in Scotland) and the lower secondary school (Year 9 in England, S2 in Scotland): these are the Progress in International Reading Literacy Study

(PIRLS) and the Trends in International Mathematics and Science Study (TIMSS), both organised by the International Association for the Evaluation of Educational Achievement (IEA). The third programme considered here, the Programme for International Student Assessment (PISA), run by the Organisation for Economic Cooperation and Development (OECD), focuses on 15-year-olds. Even though PISA is active only in the secondary sector, with no assessment of primary-age pupils, it is included here because its policy impact internationally is growing. The UK is not immune from the policy impact of PISA, and neither is its primary sector.

England's system monitoring history

Post-war to early 1970s

The UK has considerable experience of the problems and practicalities of trying to monitor the attainment of pupil populations over time, including issues concerning the interpretation of findings. The earliest attempts to assess and to monitor population attainment focused on pupils' reading ability at age 11, the end of primary schooling. In England, national attainment surveys were conducted periodically from 1948 to the late 1970s, funded by the then Department of Education and Science (DES). These relied on the repeated administration of standardised 'reading comprehension' tests at varying intervals in the monitoring period. Both of the tests used – the Watts-Vernon test and the National Survey Form 6 (NS6) – were silent reading tests, comprising 'aided' sentence completion items (i.e. children completed each sentence by selecting appropriate words from a given list), and each offering age-related norms. The 10-minute Watts-Vernon test was first developed in 1947, and comprised 35 sentences ordered in terms of difficulty (i.e. the proportion completing the sentence correctly in the standardisation exercise). It was used in attainment surveys in 1948, 1952, 1956, 1961, 1964 and 1970–71. The 20-minute NS6 was first developed in 1954, and comprised 60 sentences, also ordered in terms of anticipated difficulty. This test was used in surveys in 1955, 1960, 1970–71, 1976 and 1979 (in this last case within the first Assessment of Performance Unit English language survey – see later in this section).

Given what you know from Chapter 5 about assessment validity, you might ask yourself at this point how appropriate a sentence completion test could be for assessing 'reading comprehension'. Does the ability to complete sentences by selecting appropriate words from within given lists adequately cover what you understand by reading comprehension? Would the results of such a test be accepted today as legitimate reflections of children's reading comprehension skills? Would you use such a test in your own classroom or school? You might argue that completing sentences is a legitimate way of getting students to demonstrate reading comprehension skills. But is it the most valid way? Are there other kinds of evidence that could be sought that would complement sentence completion skills and so reflect a broader view of the ability to comprehend text? Look back at Chapter 3 if you need reminding! Certainly, the two tests came in for criticism at the time as lacking adequate construct validity. That said, what were the results of all the testing, and how were they received?

Typically, whenever national attainment appears to have risen everyone is content, particularly those politicians and education policy makers who happen to be in government at the time. Credit is claimed for initiatives of various kinds that happen to have been put in place in preceding years. Should attainment appear to be stable little comment is usually forthcoming – there are rarely protests, but there is equally rarely any rejoicing. In contrast, should attainment appear to have fallen there can be consternation, outrage and debate. Everything from the politicians of the day to the nature of the test used is identified as the reason for 'system failure' by journalists and other commentators.

According to the survey test results, reading attainment rose slightly in the immediate post-war period. So far so good. But then it began to fall away (DES 1966; Start and Wells 1972; DES 1978). As you might predict, the apparent rise in reading attainment was well received by all. But when the test results began to suggest falling standards the arguments began. There was debate about how real the apparently falling standards were, as well as about what might be done to redress the situation should the decline be genuine. The tests themselves inevitably came in for criticism. This was not only to do with whether sentence completion was the right way to assess reading comprehension. Critics also questioned whether the same test items could possibly retain relevance over time. It was acknowledged that some of the vocabulary content in the tests had become increasingly less relevant than when they were first constructed: *mannequin parade*, *wheelwright* and *haberdasher* are examples. A third problem with the NS6 was that it eventually exhibited 'ceiling effects' for 15-year-olds, meaning that the tests were not sufficiently demanding for this age group and the more able pupils were unable to demonstrate their true comprehension abilities. The tests were therefore providing an underestimate of the population's ability to comprehend text.

The government of the day, in response to this monitoring experience and the debates about standards that it fuelled, set up a Committee of Inquiry, to look into all aspects of the teaching of English in schools, and not just reading. The Bullock Committee's terms of reference were:

To consider in relation to schools:

a all aspects of teaching the use of English, including reading, writing, and speech;
b how present practice might be improved and the role that initial and in-service training might play;
c to what extent arrangements for monitoring the general level of attainment in these skills can be introduced or improved;

and to make recommendations.

DES 1975: xxxi

The Committee reflected on the cumulated experience of the existing attainment monitoring programme, and in particular on the interpretational problems associated with its results. In their influential report, *A Language for Life*, familiarly known as 'the Bullock Report', the members of the Committee outlined what they considered would be a more effective alternative methodology for attainment monitoring (DES 1975: chapter 3). The central pivot of their proposed new strategy would be a dynamic question bank. From this bank questions would be selected from survey to survey to create monitoring instruments that would be responsive to developments in the curriculum, and which would allow comparable assessments of performance over time. The bank itself would consist of a number of separate question pools, different pools being associated with different aspects of the language mode concerned. It was to be dynamic in the sense that outmoded questions would be removed from time to time, to be replaced by new questions that would be more relevant to current curricula.

And so it was that in the late 1970s the Assessment of Performance Unit (APU) survey programmes came into being in England, Wales and Northern Ireland, again funded by the then Department of Education and Science. Surveys were carried out in English language (not reading alone), mathematics and science – with foreign language and design and technology surveys appearing later as one-off exercises. Like the reading surveys that had preceded them, the new surveys focused on pupils aged 11 (end of primary education) and 15 (end of compulsory education), with age 13 added for science, since this was the last opportunity to assess population attainment before pupils made their optional subject choices for external examination preparation.

1970s to late 1980s

Each APU monitoring programme began in the late 1970s with a series of five annual cross-national surveys, moving onto a three-year cycle before being discontinued in the late 1980s when the National Curriculum was introduced and its associated assessment system launched. What form did the APU surveys take, what did they offer that the earlier reading surveys had not, what were the perceived strengths and weaknesses, and why was the programme discontinued? These are questions you will surely be asking. So let us briefly cover the ground.

All APU surveys were sample-based, that is they assessed representative samples of pupils at the respective ages in each country. And unlike the earlier reading surveys in England, APU surveys did not rely on one single test for attainment information. Numerous test items and tasks, written and practical, were prepared for administration in the surveys; these were packaged into 'tests' that were then randomly distributed among the pupils in the survey sample (this strategy is called 'matrix sampling'). Between them, the several different 'test packages' that were administered to pupils in each survey represented a very broad variety of constituent items and tasks (there were no official national curricula in operation in any of the three countries at the time). All the APU teams experimented with early forms of practical and performance assessment task in their subject areas. In addition, both pupils and teachers were invited to complete questionnaires to provide information about the learning environment, with which to contextualise the attainment results.

It was widely acknowledged that much of the materials development work of the APU teams was ground-breaking, and the impact on teaching was considerable, especially in the area of practical activities. In the field of assessment itself frontiers were also pushed, with different 'modern' measurement models being adopted in the different subject areas, though this inevitably attracted criticism on the basis of their validity for over-time attainment monitoring (Foxman et al. 1991 offer an account of this).

Full and detailed survey reports were produced. Each included attainment results, at test level and for illustrative selections of individual items and tasks, and questionnaire findings. For overviews of survey experience over the initial five-year series of annual surveys, and key findings, see Gorman et al. (1988) for English language; Foxman et al. (1985) for mathematics; Russell et al. (1988) for science at age 11, Schofield et al. (1989) for science at age 13 and Archenhold et al. (1988) for science at age 15. Johnson (1989) reviewed the science monitoring experience from a technical perspective, while Foxman et al. (1991) overviewed APU experience in general in light of the imminent introduction of the National Curriculum.

In addition to the full survey reports, the APU monitoring teams produced a series of booklets for teachers on particular aspects. Among those featuring findings for 11-year-olds are the following: MacLure and Hargreaves (1986) on the assessment of speaking and listening; White (1986) on writing assessment; Gorman and Kispal (1987) on reading assessment;

Gorman (1987) and White (1987), respectively, on pupils' attitudes to reading and to writing; Mason and Ruddock (1986) on decimals; Harlen (1983) on science at age 11; Welford *et al.* (1985) on practical testing in science; White and Welford (1988) on the use of language in science. Johnson and Murphy (1986) produced an APU 'occasional paper' on gender differences in science.

Whatever were considered to be the technical strengths and weaknesses of the APU programme as a whole, it is fair to say that the politicians of the day eventually became disillusioned with it. There were a number of reasons for their disillusionment.

Firstly, while the programmes reported attainment for various aspects in each subject – for example, 'reading' and 'oracy' in English language, 'applying science concepts' and 'observation skills' in science – none reported attainment at the level of whole subjects, which is what politicians prefer for a rapid overview of the situation. Secondly, none of the programmes showed any evidence of clearly rising attainment, and this is always bad news politically: although the mathematics programme, which was fortunate enough to have a later survey in 1987, did show some evidence of a change in the pattern of attainment (Foxman *et al.* 1990). Thirdly, the surveys were deliberately designed not to be able to report any attainment results for individual pupils nor to be able to offer any comparative information about the performance of individual schools. This was to minimise any perception on the part of teachers that they might be being evaluated, at a time when the issue of school accountability was growing in importance. Fourthly, the programmes were not able to provide the kind of information politicians eventually clamoured for, which was what pupils *specifically* 'knew' and 'could do', i.e. a level for reporting somewhere between population mean scores and individual question responses.

For example, the mathematics programme could comment on whether population attainment in mathematics as a whole had risen, fallen or remained the same over a period of time. And it could also provide information about how pupils in general performed on each of a number of individual fractions problems. But it could not offer comment of the type 'x% of 11-year-olds can successfully handle improper fractions' (how many such fractions would an individual pupil need to answer correctly to be considered to be 'successful' in 'handling fractions'?). The programme had never been designed to do this.

In response, in mid-1987, the British Government set up the Task Group for Assessment and Testing (TGAT), to look into the issues and come up with a) a national curriculum and b) a framework for assessment of that curriculum. The group was headed by Professor Paul Black, who was at the time Director of the King's College London arm of the team that designed and implemented the APU science survey programme. The group, which was under severe pressure to deliver, submitted its final report to the government at the end of 1987 (TGAT 1988), after just six months of work. The Government acted quickly on the report. So quickly that the APU teams had barely any time to attempt to amass any useful empirical evidence from the huge reservoir of attainment data that had been accumulated over several years to submit to the consultation process that took place early in 1988:

> It is not known how much account was taken of research evidence, but there was little or no time for the APU Teams to prepare a systematic comparison of their data with the proposed target levels.
>
> Foxman *et al.* 1991: 175

The APU survey programmes were summarily ended, and with the 1988 Education Reform Act the National Curriculum, along with its accompanying statutory assessment arrangements, was introduced into England and Wales. Northern Ireland followed suit under the Education Reform (Northern Ireland) Order 1989. Scotland, traditionally having independent control of its educational system, also introduced a national curriculum at around the same time, but without statutory assessment.

Late 1980s to early 1990s

The main features of the TGAT assessment recommendations were a shift in emphasis from summative assessment to formative assessment, a move (in principle) from 'absolute' standards to criterion-referenced assessment, and replacement of the idea of fixed minimum standards with a flexible 10-level progression framework spanning the numerous broadly defined 'attainment targets' (Lawton 1992). Partly to address concerns surrounding the notion of formally testing 7-year-olds and 11-year-olds, and partly to value the professionalism of teachers, it was envisaged that pupils would be assessed by their teachers. Formative assessment would become an integral part of classroom, and out-of-class, activity, where it was not so already, enabling teachers to identify learning difficulties in individual children as they arose. And to support teachers when arriving at summative level judgements, 'standard assessment tasks' (SATs) would be provided for classroom use. These were the tasks that the ex-APU teams and others soon found themselves developing.

Sadly, this early model of National Curriculum assessment was doomed to failure from the start. For what exactly were teachers expected to do under this new system, in terms of pupil assessment? 'Too much' was the answer. So much too much, in fact, that the system soon cracked (see Sainsbury 1994 for an interesting account). Here is why.

Alongside each programme of study was a set of attainment targets, which essentially structured the curriculum for that subject in terms of the relevant body of knowledge, skills and understanding. Examples are 'reading' and 'spelling' in English (or Welsh), 'using and applying mathematics', 'algebra', 'shape and space (location)' in mathematics, 'processes of life', 'forces', 'sound and music' in science. Within each attainment target a 10-level progression framework was described in the form of 'statements of attainment' (SoAs). For example, for level 3 of the attainment target 'Number (Operations)' in mathematics we have:

- know and use addition and subtraction number facts to 20 (including zero)
- solve problems involving multiplication or division of whole numbers or money, using a calculator where necessary
- know and use multiplication facts up to 5 × 5, and all those in 2, 5 and 10 multiplication tables.

The national standards reflected in the levels were to provide meaningful information to learners, their teachers, parents, carers and others about pupils' learning, so that their learning progress might be monitored in relation to their prior attainment and to expectations for learners of their age – these same expectations that remain 20 years later:

- level 2 represented expectations for the average 7-year-old
- level 4 represented expectations for the average 11-year-old
- level 5–6 represented expectations for the average 14-year-old

The progression framework was in principle a criterion-referenced framework, the statements of attainment being the criteria against which level attainment would be assessed.

Teachers were expected to assess each of their pupils against each statement of attainment, and somehow to come to decisions about appropriate levels. One immediate problem was that the number of attainment targets was large in some subjects, and there were multiple statements of attainment against each level within each of these. In particular, while English had only 5 attainment targets, mathematics had 14 and science had 17, so that between these three subjects alone there were hundreds of separate statements of attainment. The requirement to assess all of them left teachers with a very difficult, arguably impossible, job to do, as several observers noted (among them, Brown *et al.* 1996; Clarke 1997; Clarke and Gipps 1998).

Evolution since the early 1990s

During the 1990s, 'national assessment moved away from teachers' control and was transformed into written examinations in English, mathematics and science ... taken by an entire year group simultaneously' (Isaacs 2010: 323). In 1993, in response to a threatened boycott of the 'examinations', the government set up a review of the curriculum and its assessment: the 'Dearing Review' (Dearing 1993). While tests continued to feature at key stages 2 and 3 after the review, these were shorter than before, and were from then on externally marked. It was at this point also that test results at these two key stages in the three core subjects began to be used to produce school league tables, which have been regularly published since then, as well as forming the basis for over-time system monitoring at authority and national levels, despite continuing questions about validity. For a very personal reflection on the fate of the original TGAT recommendations in this evolution see Black (1998).

In 2006–07 the key stage 3 curriculum was reviewed, 'to reduce prescription, increase flexibility, ensure a smoother transition for students from key stage 2 and on to key stage 4, and improve the transmission of non-core (foundation) subjects' (Isaacs 2010: 322). The new curriculum had a stronger focus than before on numeracy, literacy, and the development of 'personal, learning and thinking skills', and was introduced in September 2008. An independent review of the primary curriculum followed in 2009 (the 'Rose Review'), with the aim of reducing achievement gaps between disadvantaged children and others. The new curriculum proposed in this review was never implemented, and so we await the outcomes of the 2011 review launched by the current government.

As far as the assessment of the National Curriculum is concerned, there have been recent changes here too. In 2008 the UK government set up the 'Expert Group on Assessment', to review the cumulated experience of National Curriculum testing, and to advise on future assessment arrangements. The group reported back in early 2009 (Expert Group on Assessment 2009), and the government accepted in full the group's recommendations. One principal recommendation was that cohort testing at key stage 3 should be discontinued, and replaced by sample-based testing. The government readily concurred with the abandonment of key stage 3 testing, having experienced grave problems with test marking and results delivery in summer 2008. But a programme of sample-based testing has not been introduced. While not a recommendation, a similar change in procedure was suggested for science only at key stage 2. The key stage 2 suggestion was implemented in full in 2010. And so we arrive at the situation described in the previous chapter, and look forward to the outcomes of the 2011 review.

For interesting overviews of the history of National Curriculum assessment from different perspectives, see Isaacs (2010), Whetton (2009), and Wyse and Torrance (2009).

The situation in Northern Ireland, Scotland and Wales

Wales and Northern Ireland

Both Wales and Northern Ireland benefited in the 1980s from participation in the APU surveys described earlier. When the APU programme was discontinued, both countries followed England in introducing a national curriculum, with cohort assessment at the same key stages. However, the national curriculum in each of these two countries differed in some respects from that in England, as noted in Chapter 6. Also, in Northern Ireland there was never any test-based assessment at key stage 2, given that the 11+ was still in operation in that country.

Now that both countries have abandoned test-based assessment at key stages 2 and 3, teacher judgement will be the basis for system evaluation in each country at both key stages. For system evaluation at the end of obligatory schooling, both countries are now also looking to the OECD PISA project for information (see later section).

Scotland

Like England, Scotland has a long history of system evaluation, with surveys of the attainment of 10-year-olds in English and arithmetic – the 'Scottish Scholastic Survey' – having been conducted as far back as 1953, and repeated in 1963 (SCRE 1968). In 1953 the whole population of 10-year-olds was tested ('cohort assessment'), while in 1963 a seven per cent sample was used. Counter to expectations, apparently, the evidence from the surveys was that pupils had improved their attainment in both areas in the intervening period.

Scotland is one of the few countries around the world, and the only one in the UK, to have retained sample-based attainment monitoring for system evaluation. The Assessment of Achievement Programme (AAP) (Condie *et al.* 2003) was launched in the mid-1980s, modelled to some extent on the APU survey programme that was already operating in the rest of the UK. Mathematics, science and English language were assessed on a three-year cycle, at three key stages, namely P4, P7 and S2 (nine-year-olds, 12-year-olds and 14-year olds). When the 5–14 curriculum was introduced into the country in the early 1990s, Scotland, unlike England in the late 1980s, did not abandon its survey programme. It adapted it, so that the surveys newly reported pupil attainment with reference to the same 5–14 curriculum attainment levels that teachers were themselves using in the classroom (see SOED 1991a for English language, SOED 1991b and SOEID 1999 for mathematics, and SOED 1993 for science).

Following a national consultation on assessment in the early 2000s, the AAP was rebranded as the Scottish Survey of Achievement (SSA), taking on a broader remit to assess and report attainment in key subjects at local education authority level as well as nationally. By this time the AAP had changed its key stage emphasis from P4, P7 and S2 to P3, P5, P7 and S2 (i.e. eight-year-olds, 10-year olds, 12-year olds and 14-year olds). The SSA continued the pattern (for the last survey report in the SSA series, see Scottish Government 2010b).

The recent introduction of the 'Curriculum for Excellence' (CfE) (Scottish Government 2010a) has not led to the abandonment of sample-based monitoring in this country either. But once again there has been a rebranding. The survey programme is now called the Scottish Survey of Literacy and Numeracy (SSLN). As its name implies, the new programme is to look at attainment in English and numeracy only, in alternate years, reporting attainment against CfE levels. The stage focus has shifted back to P4, P7 and S2.

In addition to benefiting from its own sample-based survey programme, Scotland has regularly taken part in all the international survey programmes, namely TIMSS, PIRLS and PISA.

In 2011, exceptionally, Scotland decided not to participate in TIMSS and PIRLS, which both took place that year, to relieve what would have been undue pressure on its schools, especially in the secondary sector, thus giving priority to the SSLN.

International comparative surveys: TIMSS and PIRLS

The International Association for the Evaluation of Educational Achievement (IEA) has been conducting international surveys in reading, mathematics and science for over half a century. The organisation was founded more than 50 years ago, in 1959, by a small group of leading educational researchers, with the intention of carrying out cross-border attainment surveys. National surveys had repeatedly shown pupil-based factors, especially socioeconomic background, strongly outweighing school-based factors in correlation studies, so that it was difficult to provide any evidence that schools 'made a difference'. It was hoped that looking across borders would provide richer information with which to explore the issue of school impact (Husen and Postlethwaite 1996), since this would introduce greater heterogeneity into educational provision:

> The world could be conceived as a huge educational laboratory where different national practices lent themselves to comparison that could yield new insights into determinants of educational outcomes.
>
> Purves 1991: 34

Reports on the early surveys focused heavily on presenting and interpreting the results of 'impact analyses', that is analyses aimed at exploring relationships between pupils' test performances and pupil-based, school-based and system-based factors. Little emphasis was given to the relative standing of specific named countries, as this was not of primary research interest. But things have changed. From its original conception as a research tool, of interest principally to educational researchers, the political significance of the IEA has inevitably and steadily increased. Survey reports and press releases now give prominence to 'country league tables' showing the relative standing of every participating country in terms of its sample pupils' performances, and this is the information that politicians and policy makers look for first (for an example see Mullis *et al.* 2003 and Hilton 2006).

The IEA's two major survey programmes currently are the Progress in International Reading Literacy Study (PIRLS), which has been running on a five-year cycle since 2001, and the Trends in International Mathematics and Science Study (TIMSS), which has been running on a four-year cycle since 1995. Both programmes were actually preceded on an ad hoc basis by surveys of the relevant subjects.

One important feature of both programmes since their regular cycles began is that they report pupil attainment on a 'stretched' score scale, that is one engineered to have a mean score of 500 and a standard deviation of 100 (a standard deviation is a conventional measure of 'spread' in a distribution of scores, technically the square root of the variance). Pupil scores, and in turn country average scores, are located on the scale by using a probability-based item response theory (IRT) application. We touched on IRT very briefly in Chapter 4, you might remember. What is important to note here is that in practice each pupil tested will have attempted at most two pencil-and-paper tests, containing around 30 items per subject.

From its earliest beginnings, the IEA has focused its surveys on 10-year-olds and, though for mathematics and science only, 14-year-olds. In each age group in each participating country, nationally representative samples of 3,500 to 4,000 pupils are selected for testing.

The pupil samples are created by first randomly selecting a sample of schools (controlling for characteristics like size, location and socioeconomic composition, i.e. by 'stratifying' the population of schools before making selections), and then by taking one class, or occasionally two classes, of pupils from the relevant year-group in each school. In addition to taking tests, pupils also answer questionnaires designed to gather information about their backgrounds, subject attitudes and interests, and about their classroom experiences, among other topics. Teachers complete questionnaires, too, about issues such as subject provision and curriculum coverage, as well as providing demographic information.

In England fewer than 150 primary schools are typically selected each time for participation in an IEA survey. So the chances that your school will be selected are low, and extremely low for selection in consecutive surveys. If your school *is* ever chosen for participation, and if you are the school's assessment coordinator, then most of the additional work involved in conducting the survey in your school will come your way. But do not be put off by the thought of this extra workload. Consider the occasion an opportunity – a rare opportunity – to see the tests used in the surveys at first hand, and to witness how your 10-year-old pupils react to them.

In the meantime, let's look at each programme in turn, starting with the most historic programme, which is TIMSS.

TIMSS

The IEA's first sample-based mathematics survey took place in the early 1960s and involved 12 countries (Wilson and Peaker 1971). The form of that first survey was already comprehensive, and clearly in line with the founding philosophy and intentions of the association. Pupil performance was assessed for a number of different aspects of school mathematics, and in addition a large volume of information was gathered about circumstances of learning: school organisation, curriculum and teaching methods, and social factors. The first science survey took place around a decade later, and was similarly ambitious (Comber and Keeves 1973).

During the 35 years since that pioneering first survey numerous, even larger-scale, more ambitious surveys have been conducted in mathematics and science, with the participation of developing as well as developed countries (Johnson 1999). The third set of surveys, the 'Third International Mathematics and Science Surveys' (TIMSS) took place in 1995. A total of 45 countries around the world participated, and several reports were produced: for the results for 10-year-olds see Martin *et al.* (1997) and Mullis *et al.* (1997). Harmon *et al.* (1997) report the findings from performance assessments. Before the next round of surveys took place, in 1999, a fixed four-year survey cycle had been agreed, putting the programme on a sounder footing than before, and 'TIMSS' came to stand for 'Trends in International Mathematics and Science Study'. Further TIMSS surveys took place in 2003, 2007 (the latest survey to be reported at the time of writing) and 2011.

A principal aim in TIMSS, apart from assessing the achievement of pupils, is to provide contextual information that could help in the interpretation of attainment findings, which include cross-border differences in achievement and within-country differences in the achievement of pupil subgroups, such as boys and girls. To this end the programme investigates not just the 'intended' curriculum in each country, that is the curriculum as recorded officially in programmes of study, but also the 'implemented' curriculum, that is the curriculum actually delivered in classrooms (what, how and by whom), as well as the 'achieved' curriculum, as reflected in pupil achievement.

Both the mathematics and the science surveys use a roughly equal mixture of multiple-choice and constructed response questions, classified into 'knowing', 'applying' and 'reasoning' (an adaptation of Bloom's taxonomy, as you will recognise from Chapter 4). Within each subject area the questions for 10-year-olds span three content domains: in science these are 'physical science', 'life science' and 'earth science'; in mathematics we have 'data display', 'geometric shapes and measures' and 'number'. In 2007, reflecting the pattern in previous surveys, just over 350 different test items were administered in the primary survey; in science items tended to be grouped into tasks that shared the same stimulus material, to some extent following the pattern of reading comprehension tests. Tasks and items were distributed among pupils using matrix sampling. Each child in the survey took a maths test and a science test, together lasting a total of 72 minutes, with a pause between. In addition there was a short questionnaire.

England participated in the TIMSS surveys of 1995 (see Keys *et al.* 1996a, b), 1999 (when it failed to reach sampling quality criteria), 2003 (Ruddock *et al.* 2004), 2007 (Sturman *et al.* 2008a) and 2011, and Scotland took part in 1995, 2003 and 2007 (Horne *et al.* 2008). What, then, can we say about the performances of England and Scotland?

According to its TIMSS results, England is apparently among the highest performing countries in the world in both mathematics and science in Year 5, with 2007 scale scores of 541 for maths and 542 for science – essentially the same, and certainly substantially higher than the overall country average of 500 (Sturman *et al.* 2008a, 2008b). Mathematics attainment increased from one survey to another (1995, 2003, 2007), while in science the attainment increase happened between 1995 and 2003. There were no marked differences in either subject in pupils' average performances in 'knowing', 'applying' and 'reasoning', and there was also a relatively flat profile across the three science content areas.

In mathematics, pupils were weaker in general on 'number', particularly 'computation', than on 'data display' and 'geometric shapes and measures' (but note that we have no idea of either the validity or the reliability of performance reports for these subdomains). In each subject, around 15 per cent of pupils were estimated to be in the top 10 per cent of performers (scale scores at or above 625). There were no overall gender differences in either maths or science.

As far as pupil attitudes to maths and science are concerned, around 60 per cent of Year 5 pupils were found to have highly positive attitudes to each subject, although in both cases the proportion had dropped since 1995. A higher proportion of pupils had a high level of confidence in learning mathematics than in learning science (64 per cent compared with 55 per cent), with substantially higher proportions of boys than girls claiming high confidence (Sturman 2008b: 7–8).

Scotland's P5 performance was at the overall country average in 2007 in both subjects, showing relative stability since the 1995 survey in maths, and since 2003 in science after a fall between 1995 and 2003 (Horne *et al.* 2008). Bearing in mind the comments made earlier about the unknown validity and reliability of subdomain scores, in mathematics Scottish performance was higher in 'data display' than in 'geometric shapes and measures', and higher in the latter than in 'number', while in science performance was better in 'earth science' than in 'life science', and better in the latter than in 'physical science'. There was a gender difference in mathematics at P5, in favour of boys (though only of nine points, which could in practice translate to less than one test item on average). There was no overall gender difference in science. As to subject attitudes, 70 per cent of P5 pupils reported enjoying science, and over 60 per cent reported a high level of confidence in learning science (Horne *et al.* 2008: 11).

As noted earlier, while England also took part in TIMSS 2011, Scotland chose not to participate on this occasion (nor in PIRLS), to give priority to its own survey programme, the SSLN.

PIRLS

PIRLS surveys are on a five-year cycle, and focus on 10-year-olds. The first survey in 2001 was based on the following definition of 'reading ability':

> the ability to understand and use those written language forms required by society and/or valued by the individual. Young readers can construct meaning from a variety of texts. They read to learn, to participate in communities of readers, and for enjoyment.
>
> Campbell *et al.* 2001: 3

Test creation is underpinned by two 'reading purposes':

- reading for literacy experience
- reading to acquire and use information.

and four 'comprehension processes':

- focus on and retrieve explicitly stated information (20 per cent of marks)
- make straightforward inferences (30 per cent of marks)
- interpret and integrate ideas and information (30 per cent of marks)
- examine and evaluate content, language and textual elements (20 per cent of marks).

A number of different short reading comprehension tests have been administered in each survey, some tests being carried forward from one survey to another for comparability purposes. In the 2006 survey, for example, there were 10 tests, five with narrative source texts and five with informational texts, each with around 12 test questions. Two tests of each type were carried forward from the 2001 survey. The tests were randomly distributed among the sample pupils, using matrix sampling. Each pupil took two tests, one of each type, together lasting around 80 minutes with a pause between, and a 15–30 minute questionnaire. Test questions carried up to three marks each, so that an individual pupil would have a maximum test score of around 25 marks.

A total of 35 different countries around the world participated in the first PIRLS survey in 2001 (Mullis *et al.* 2003, 2004); in 2006 the number rose above 40, and rose again to over 50 in 2011. As in TIMSS, all test materials, originally in English, are translated into many different world languages – 45 languages in 2006! If you have any translation experience, you might ask yourself whether the need to use translated materials in reading surveys could have an effect on attainment in some or all countries.

Results from the first two surveys have proved difficult to interpret. For example, while England's 'score' in 2001 was 553, putting it in third place among the participating countries, it fell to 539 in 2006, and its league table position plummeted to 19th (see the national reports for England – Twist *et al.* 2003 and 2007). Scotland, meanwhile, achieved a 'score' of 528 in 2001, and showed an essentially unchanged performance in 2006, with a score of 527 (Scottish Government 2007). Yet it dropped from 14th in the league table in 2001 to 26th in 2006! Rank orders, of course, have limited meaning in this kind of context. Differences of one or two points on the stretched scale could shift a country from one position to another. And when different countries, and different numbers of countries, participate each time then rank orders will inevitably fluctuate relatively arbitrarily. What does it all mean? Perhaps the 2011 results will clarify the picture.

Clearer, and more believable, findings have emerged from the PIRLS questionnaire enquiries. In particular, strong gender differences have emerged across the board in favour of girls, both for reading attainment and for attitudes to reading, confirming previous findings in other contexts:

> Girls consistently outperform boys in reading assessments. In the national tests in England at the end of key stage 2 (age 11), annually about eight per cent more girls than boys achieve at least the target level. A report published by the DfES (2007) summarised data on the so-called 'gender gap'. It was reported that the gender gap was evident in English from the outcomes of the Foundation stage (age 5) through to GCSE (age 16) and that it was most evident at key stages 3 and 4 (11–16).
>
> Twist *et al.* 2007: 17

In Scotland, too, national assessment surveys have consistently shown girls to produce better performances than boys in reading – and in writing – at all ages tested; for the latest report see Scottish Government 2010b.

The OECD PISA programme

'PISA' (the Programme for International Student Assessment) was launched in 2000, with the primary purpose of providing the OECD with comparative information about the output of its member countries' educational systems, in terms of pupil attainment at age 15 (the end of obligatory schooling in many countries). Information about every other aspect of educational provision – structure, input and process – had been regularly documented in the OECD's periodic *Education at a Glance* reports, but no complementary information about outcomes was available to complete the comparative picture. Where countries had domestic attainment survey programmes in place, these took different forms with different methods of reporting, and did not in every case assess pupil attainment at age 15. They therefore had minimal, if any, potential for facilitating cross-border comparisons. And so PISA was born.

PISA surveys take place on a 3-year cycle, and are intended to transcend national curricula by assessing 'skills for life':

- *Reading literacy*
  An individual's capacity to: understand, use, reflect on and engage with written texts, in order to achieve one's goals, to develop one's knowledge and potential, and to participate in society.

- *Mathematical literacy*
  An individual's capacity to identify and understand the role that mathematics plays in the world, to make well-founded judgements and to use and engage with mathematics in ways that meet the needs of that individual's life as a constructive, concerned and reflective citizen.

- *Scientific literacy*
  An individual's scientific knowledge and use of that knowledge to identify questions, to acquire new knowledge, to explain scientific phenomena, and to draw evidence-based conclusions about science-related issues, understanding of the characteristic features of science as a form of human knowledge and enquiry, awareness of how science and technology shape our material, intellectual, and cultural environments, and willingness to engage in science-related issues, and with the ideas of science, as a reflective citizen.

OECD 2009: 14

Every survey incorporates assessment of all three literacies. On each occasion, one type of literacy assumes 'major domain' status, and consumes two-thirds or more of the testing space, while the other two literacies are 'minor domains'. Each type of literacy is assessed as a major domain in every third survey, i.e. every nine years. The latest survey to date is that of 2009, which for the first time has been able to offer comparisons of countries' standing over time for the same 'major domain', i.e. reading literacy. The next survey will be in 2012, when mathematics will be the major domain, allowing comparison with 2003, with science following in 2015, allowing comparison with 2006.

The first survey report, and in particular the country 'league table' presented within it, caused more than a flurry of interest among politicians and policy makers around the world. It offered satisfaction to those whose countries appeared towards the top of the league table (notably Finland among European countries, along with several Asian countries, including Japan and Korea), inspired resignation in those whose countries were placed towards the bottom, and surprised and dismayed some of those whose countries performed much less well than expected when compared with other countries with similar states of socioeconomic development. There was indeed 'PISA shock' in some cases. Inevitably, this league table interest has been maintained as further surveys have been reported.

The results of the surveys for the UK and its constituent countries are shown in Table 7.1 (the UK, as a single OECD country, is reported as a whole in PISA reports, constituent country results being produced by the UK itself).

Both England and Scotland showed performances that were significantly above those of the OECD at large in reading in 2000 (Gill *et al.* 2002, SEED 2002) and in science in 2006 (Bradshaw *et al.* 2007a; Scottish Government 2007). Scotland showed higher than average performance also in mathematics in 2003 (Thorpe 2004); in that year the UK's results were not published, because severe difficulties in recruiting sufficient numbers of schools in England meant that the OECD's strict sampling criteria were not met. In 2009 both countries' performances were close to the OECD average in reading literacy (Bradshaw *et al.* 2010a; Scottish Government 2010c).

Neither Northern Ireland nor Wales participated in the PISA survey of 2000. While they did participate in 2003, they did so as a part of the UK, and were disqualified along with England because of England's sampling difficulties. When results did finally become available for these two countries (Bradshaw *et al.* 2007a, b, 2010b, c), they showed that in 2006 both Northern Ireland and Wales produced science performances below those of England and Scotland, with Wales dropping particularly low for reading in 2009.

PISA has already had a number of important impacts on countries within and outside the OECD. Long-established system structures, which until PISA had been assumed to function satisfactorily, have suddenly been under review. Germany is an example, with its segregated academic/vocational education system.

Table 7.1 Mean scores in PISA 'major domains' in 2000, 2003, 2006, 2009

	Reading 2000*	Maths 2003**	Science 2006	Reading 2009
United Kingdom	523	–	515	494
England	523	–	516	495
Northern Ireland	–	–	508	499
Scotland	526	524	515	500
Wales	–	–	505	476
OECD	500	500	500	493
Total countries and economies	32 (27 OECD)	41 (30 OECD)	57 (30 OECD)	65 (34 OECD)

Sources: Gill et al. 2002; SEED 2002; Thorpe 2004; Bradshaw *et al.* 2007a, b, 2010a, b; Scottish Government 2007, 2010c; standard errors are included in the survey reports – these indicate the precision of the estimates.

Notes
* Northern Ireland and Wales were not included in the UK's sample in 2000.
** The UK failed to meet the OECD's tight sampling quality criteria in 2003, and so its results were not published that year; Scotland was able to produce its own result.

Some countries have already taken steps to develop and implement national or regional curricula to replace the variety of more localised curricula that existed before. One example is Switzerland, which is in the process of replacing numerous cantonal curricula with a common curriculum for each major linguistic region. Other countries have looked with fresh eyes at historic practices within their education systems, and are witnessing growing calls for change to address what is seen as worryingly inadequate attainment results in PISA. France, for example, is questioning its long-standing practice of '*redoublement*', where sizeable proportions of pupils – almost half – are required to repeat one or more years of their secondary schooling because of poor test results (Mons and Pons 2010).

Then there is the issue of attainment monitoring for accountability purposes. In a direct response to PISA, many of those countries that have no tradition of formalised educational evaluation have recently or are in the process of launching their own attainment monitoring programmes.

The UK has not been immune to the impact of the international surveys. Indeed, the latest National Curriculum review in England has been at least partly triggered by pupil attainment and curriculum comparisons with those of other participant countries (Oates 2010).

Questions for reflection

• By the time this book is published the results of the 2011 National Curriculum review in England will be known. In your view, are the changes that will be introduced in the next few years, both to the curriculum itself and to its assessment, positive or negative ones? Can you explain your views?

• Teacher assessment is an essential ingredient in classroom life. But there are issues to do with using teacher summative assessment for system evaluation. Can you identify what these might be? What are the pros and cons? And what is your conclusion about the validity of using teacher assessment for this purpose?

- A handful of the results from the IEA surveys have been included in this chapter, for England and Scotland. Did they surprise you, if this is the first time you have seen them? How do you think participation in such surveys benefits governments, if it does? If your own country has not yet participated, would you urge your own politicians to think about 'joining up', given the financial costs involved?
- The PISA programme attempts to assess 'life skills', and minimises any direct link to secondary school curricula. Do you think it's possible meaningfully to assess 15-year-olds without a curriculum link? And if it can be done, how reasonable do you think it is that the results of testing 15-year-olds should impact so widely and so seriously on primary education around the world? Explain!

Further reading

Foxman, D., Hutchison, D. and Bloomfield, B. (1991) *The APU Experience. 1977–1990,* London: Schools Examinations and Assessment Council.

Greaney, V. and Kellaghan, T. (2008) *Assessing National Achievement Levels in Education*, Washington: The World Bank.

Johnson, S. (1989) *Monitoring Science Performance: The APU Experience*, London: HMSO.

Whetton, C. (2009) 'A Brief History of a Testing Time: National Curriculum Assessment in England 1989–2008', *Educational Research*, 51: 137–59.

Chapter 8

Using assessment results for evaluation

Chapter 8 considers in turn each of the major areas of evaluation which rely in part or whole on the use and interpretation of the results of pupil assessment: pupil evaluation, teacher and school self-evaluation and external evaluation, system evaluation, and programme evaluation. Final comments are offered on the importance of achieving assessment literacy on the part of those groups of professionals identified in Chapter 1, namely class teachers, assessment coordinators, headteachers and local authority subject advisers.

We have seen that pupil assessment can be carried out in many different ways, often without the pupil even knowing that assessment is taking place. We talk with children, we ask them questions, we watch them at play and at work, we see the products that they produce, and, ultimately, we might give them tests. When we have assessment evidence, whether from a one-off test or cumulated over a period of informal interaction, we use that information to make decisions about the child. Sometimes, as in formative assessment, this happens implicitly, but at other times it happens explicitly. This is where assessment turns into evaluation. The result of the evaluation has immediate implications for the individual child, but the consequences can be broader than this. Taken jointly, the results of individual pupil evaluations often feed up into higher-level group evaluations that can affect you and your school, as well as the educational system as a whole. We therefore need not only to be concerned about the validity and reliability of assessment-based decisions for our own pupils, we need also to understand how these results are put to use by others later.

Pupil evaluation

Pupil assessment, and its evaluation, might be diagnostic, in which case we use the assessment results to tell us where a pupil's learning strengths and weaknesses are: which facts have been learned and which not, which concepts have been understood and which not, which skills have been acquired and which not, or not securely. Armed with this information we can determine the best course of action for the pupil, in terms of what needs to be done next to remedy any gaps. This is the kind of use made of assessment results in 'formative assessment', where the child is temporarily, frequently and usually unobtrusively assessed and evaluated, in order that progress in learning can be continuously checked and maximised before any formal assessment takes place later.

In this kind of ongoing informal assessment the criteria with which a pupil's performance is being judged will be different from one occasion to another, but the criteria should always be quite clear, since they will be, or should be, closely tied to what is being taught and learned at that particular time. It is sometimes claimed that we needn't worry too much about validity and reliability for this kind of assessment. But that is not true. It is particularly not true if at some future point you, the teacher, are to be expected to arrive at summative judgements of your pupils' learning, using a set of given criteria that all teachers should be applying in the same way. If your ongoing in-class assessments, however you make them, bear little relation to future shared goals for learning, then the validity of your summative judgements in relation to those future goals could be in doubt. Your pupils could be the ones to suffer.

But what are these criteria that could be used to make judgements about a child on the basis of a summative assessment? How do we identify a pupil as being at this level of attainment or this other, or in this group or that one for some future purpose? How do we use assessment evidence to label a child as 'level 2' in mathematics rather than level 3 or level 1, or 'secure at 1st level' in literacy as opposed to being 'insecure'? A limited number of approaches are adopted to address this challenge.

If teachers are expected to make judgements about a child's location in some progressive achievement framework, then it is common to provide verbal 'level descriptions' for this purpose, such as those discussed in Chapter 6 in relation to England's current National Curriculum assessment (see also Appendix 2). If, on the other hand, grouping decisions of this kind are to be made on the basis of test results, then we typically appeal to 'cut scores' to separate one group from another, or we arbitrarily decide on proportions of the pupil group that we will simply label in a certain way. So we might decide that 'very secure' performance in reading will be confirmed when the pupil achieves a test score of 80 per cent or more. Or, we might instead simply agree that the 'very secure' readers are those in the top 10 per cent of test performers, i.e. those 10 per cent of pupils with the highest test scores. You will remember from Chapter 4 that the first two examples, i.e. teacher judgement using level descriptors and pupil classification on the basis of given test scores, are examples of criterion-referenced assessment, while the last example, simply separating off the top 10 per cent of pupils on the basis of their test performances, is an example of norm-referenced assessment.

Whichever approach we adopt, we must be able to explain our rationale for using it, and be able to justify it to others. We need to establish the authenticity of verbal achievement descriptors, and the validity of chosen cut scores or cutting proportions. Otherwise, the results of the assessment and subsequent evaluation would not be transparent and could be flawed. The outcome might sometimes lead to unjustified and at times unfortunate consequences, not only for the pupils who are wrongfully or arbitrarily judged, but also for their teachers and schools, when they are in turn evaluated on the basis of their pupils' results.

Whenever you are asked to make summative judgements using written criteria, and whenever you use a test to categorise your pupils in some way by applying cut scores, do not take the criteria at face value. Ask yourself what meaning they are intended to have, and what meaning they actually have in your opinion. Try to find out how the criteria were arrived at – by whom, when, and using what procedure. Whether you find answers or not, you might nevertheless be constrained to apply the criteria as best you can. At worst, you will become aware that there might be weaknesses in the system, weaknesses that will permeate up all the higher levels of evaluation that are fundamentally based on those pupil attainment results produced in your classroom.

Teacher and school evaluation

Self-evaluation

As a class teacher you will be constantly evaluating your own teaching effectiveness, often subconsciously, as you teach and assess your pupils. You will be diagnosing learning weak spots continually throughout the year, so that you can address these quickly. And you will also note learning strengths that need no action other than progress to the next stage of learning that will build on those strengths. Both weaknesses and strengths in learning success give you invaluable feedback not only on your pupils' capabilities and effort, but also on the effectiveness of your own teaching. Over time, after you have taught several different groups of pupils you will begin to be able to distinguish the learning weaknesses that can be attributed to the pupils from those that you might attribute to yourself as their teacher. If you think improvements are necessary, then you might start experimenting, changing your teaching style perhaps, or redistributing the time given to different topics, concepts and class activities in your teaching programme. You will observe the effects of the changes, evaluating yourself.

Headteachers do something similar in their school self-evaluation, except that they look at a broader range of evidence about the functioning of the school than you will be doing in your own class-based self-evaluation. There will be financial matters to cover, administrative efficiency to consider, and the school's provision of curriculum and extra-curricular activities to monitor, amongst other matters. Pupil behaviour and attainment will feature in the list of evaluation criteria, and this is where your headteacher will be implicitly evaluating you, and all the other class teachers in the school, as a contributor to the situation. You might be entirely at ease with this thought, since it is quite proper that the school be evaluated in all critical areas. A problem might only arise for you if at some point in time you find yourself with a challenging class to manage and teach, whose behaviour and attainment results are not ideal, and you fear that these might reflect badly on you when you are personally judged.

Evaluation for accountability

When schools are evaluated by others, and the 'others' are school inspectors, authority policy makers or government politicians, then we move into the area that has in the UK become disparagingly known as 'accountability'. In Chapter 7 it was noted that school league tables were first introduced into the UK on the tails of the National Curriculum and assessment revisions in the mid-1990s. They were unpopular with most practitioners from the start, and there was a sigh of relief in many circles when cohort testing and the consequent provision of school-level results were abandoned at key stage 3 in 2007 and in science at key stage 2 in 2010.

Putting aside the emotional and political issues surrounding school league tables and school-level performance comparisons generally, there are some interpretational problems, too, that should not go unconsidered. One of these naturally concerns the attainment data that form the basis of the comparisons, and how well the data meet the accountability purpose. What kinds of test were used? How valid were these as tools for measuring what they purported to measure, whether this was reading ability, or numeracy, or science knowledge? How reliable were they for individual pupil assessment? If all is well on that front, there remains a further issue that has to do with the size of a school and the stability of its catchment in terms of its social characteristics. Where a school's catchment varies from one year to another in terms, for example, of socioeconomic background, this will clearly impact on the school's apparent relative achievement. When a school is small, then just one or two pupils in any one year could affect the school's average attainment score. Caution is always needed in school-level comparisons.

System evaluation

System evaluation is an essential activity for a modern government to engage in. It can take many forms, each with its own benefits and costs and associated issues. We have looked in Chapter 7 at examples of system evaluation that are based on pupil testing. These include: the sample-based APU survey programme that ran in England, Wales and Northern Ireland through the 1980s, until the National Curriculum was introduced; Scotland's sample-based survey programmes that have continued to operate under one name or another since the mid-1980s; the census-based National Curriculum assessment programme that has been functioning in England since the mid-1990s (and in Wales and Northern Ireland until both countries abandoned this style quite recently, opting instead for teacher assessment); and the sample-based cross-national survey programmes carried out under the aegis of the IEA since the 1960s and by the OECD since 2000.

The quality and value of system evaluation, whatever kind this might be, depends critically on a number of factors, including: the quality of the assessment materials used – their validity and reliability; the degree of curriculum coverage, or of 'life skills' representation, embodied in the totality of those assessment materials; the validity of the criteria used to make judgements about individual pupils when categorising them in some way; and, in sample-based programmes, the size and representativeness of the sample of pupils assessed, along with the pupils' degree of motivation for what is to them low stakes assessment. Stakeholders using the results of pupil testing, or of teachers' summative assessment of their pupils, should always ask questions about these issues when they set about interpreting the findings, especially when the result of this interpretation could lead to a policy action as serious as curriculum reform.

Programme evaluation

When the evaluation is of a new programme of study, or a different style of teaching, or a new activity pack for pupils, especially, but not only, when the evaluation is comparative, there are even more aspects to consider when judging whether the conclusions of the evaluation are sound. These have to do with the concept of a 'fair test', a concept you will be spending quite a lot of class time helping your pupils to acquire through the science investigations they undertake in your classroom.

If the evaluation study is wholly or partly assessment-based, then you should pay attention to all of the usual matters: the validity and reliability of the test that was used or of the teacher judgements that were made; the validity of the criteria used for slotting pupils into one group or another on the basis of their assessment results – for example into reading ages, or performance groups, or 'level 2'; and the comparative representativeness of the samples of pupils that were tested – for even when whole schools participate the pupils they provide will be samples of the larger target population that the new programme is intended for or with whom the alternative teaching style will be adopted.

In addition, however, you will also now need to think about the conditions under which the assessment took place – when, by whom and how – and about the conditions under which the programme or style was used. If, for example, the teaching programme was synthetic phonics, then you would not expect the 'synthetic phonics pupils' to be simultaneously bene-fiting from another early reading approach that the effectiveness of synthetic phonics was being evaluated against!

Final comments: the importance of achieving assessment literacy

Assessment is an essential element in every level of education, from primary to tertiary education, both for monitoring individual progress to ensure that learning is effective and for confirming the achievements of that learning at key points in the system. It is essential, there-fore, that every education professional has a basic understanding of the important assessment concepts, to be able to engage meaningfully in assessment as well as to be able to evaluate the quality of the assessment results provided by others for whatever purpose. The increasing politicisation of assessment over recent decades has strengthened this need for a high degree of assessment literacy among practitioners and others involved in the business of education.

If you are a class teacher, try to make your assessments as valid as they can be in terms of the criteria you are in principle judging your pupils against, and the criteria that they will be judged against by others later. And do your best to make your assessments fair to all your pupils, maintaining your guard against the risk of bias should you be tempted to give credit for good behaviour, effort, tidiness, or whatever, when arriving at your summative judge-ments. When you make your own tests, and when you use other tests in your class, that were chosen perhaps by your assessment coordinator or provided by your authority, evaluate those tests in terms of what they are ostensibly claiming to measure – evaluate their validity, in other words – using the criteria you have learned about in Chapters 3, 4 and 5. Do not be afraid to ask questions when you feel that a test you are required to use is less than adequate for the purpose.

If you are an assessment coordinator you need equally to have enough assessment knowl-edge and understanding to be able to evaluate any tests that you are invited to adopt for use in your school. How valid do they appear to be to you for assessing what they claim to be able to measure? What evidence is presented about their technical reliability? Is the reliability index quoted the most appropriate one given the way that the test is intended to be used? If norms are included, find out how recently these were established, and how: what kind of pupil sample was the test standardised with, how large was it and how was it selected – how representative would you say the standardisation sample was in terms of the pupils you are about to use the test with?

If you are a headteacher, then ensure that your own assessment understanding is up to scratch, given all of the assessment-based data that you use on a regular basis in your own school self-evaluation, and in your teacher evaluation. But think of your staff as well. Make CPD opportunities in assessment available to your teaching staff, whatever their age and length of teaching experience, to give them the support they need to reach an appropriate level of assessment literacy and to maintain that level. If there are few appropriate CPD courses available in your authority then put pressure on the authority to provide more. And carry out your own evaluation of the effectiveness of any CPD your staff in principle benefit from, to ensure that the time out of class has been worth the cost.

If you are an authority subject adviser then you need to keep yourself updated on assess-ment matters, and fight for the necessary resources from your authority to provide that essential CPD support in assessment that the teachers in your schools need. Keep updated also on what is happening in the international survey programmes, so that you can inform practitioners and others in your authority about these and about their findings. Encourage schools selected in your national samples to participate, to avoid the situation where the effort made by schools that do participate will not be wasted should sampling numbers be too low and survey results remain unpublished.

If you are a policy maker, working in assessment in your local authority or central government, you, too, need to be assessment literate if you are to use the results of assessment intelligently yourself in school accountability exercises or system evaluation. And you will be able to use the confidence that comes from a sound understanding to try to guide your politicians to sensible interpretations of assessment-based evidence when reviewing the findings from national and international survey programmes, and when evaluating the benefits to the country of participating in these given the significant financial costs that are usually involved.

Questions for reflection

*   Think of the last time you evaluated your own pupils, and the approach that you used in your evaluation. What would you say about the validity of the process, your involvement in it, and the fairness of the outcomes for your pupils?
*   School league tables are of great appeal to local and national policy makers and politicians. What do you see as their attraction, and what can you say about their inherent value for improving the education system?
*   System evaluation can be sample-based or can involve cohort testing. It can alternatively rely on the gathering of teachers' judgements about their pupils' achievement levels. And it can be within-country or across borders. If you were or are a policy maker, what would you say are the advantages and disadvantages of these different approaches?
*   Your school or authority is contemplating adopting a new standardised reading test for use in system and school self-evaluation, or an innovative numeracy package that offers great promise for raising pupil achievement in this area. If you were responsible for making the decision to adopt or not, how would you set about doing it?

Further reading

Cross, A. (2006) 'Looking for Patterns in OfStEd Judgements about Primary Pupil Achievement in Design and Technology', *Education 3–13*, 34: 163–72.

Croxford, L., Grek, S. and Shaik, F.J. (2009) 'Quality Assurance and Evaluation (QAE) in Scotland: Promoting Self-evaluation Within and Beyond the Country', *Journal of Education Policy*, 24: 179–93.

Harlen, W. (2007) *Assessment of Learning,* London: Sage.

Kellaghan, T., Greaney, V. and Murray, T.S. (2009) *Using the Results of a National Assessment of Educational Achievement*, Washington: The World Bank.

Ozga, J. (2009) 'Governing Education through Data in England: From Regulation to Self-evaluation', *Journal of Education Policy*, 24: 149–62.

Appendix 1

The English National Curriculum

Programmes of study for the core subjects of English, mathematics and science

The tables in this appendix offer skeletal outlines of the programmes of study for English, mathematics and science as these applied in 2011. For full curriculum details you should consult the relevant curriculum documents: DfEE/QCA 1999a (English), 1999b (Mathematics), 1999c (Science). Note also that these curricula are likely to be replaced from September 2013.

English

Table A1.1 provides a skeletal overview of the programmes of study for English for key stages 1 and 2.

Table A1.1 Skeletal outline of the key stage 1 and 2 programmes of study for English*

Speaking and listening	Speaking
	Listening
	Group discussion and interaction
	Drama
	Standard English
	Language variation
Reading	Reading strategies
	(Understanding texts)
	Reading for information
	Literature
	(Non-fiction and non-literary texts)
	Language structure and variation
Writing	Composition
	Planning and drafting
	Punctuation
	Spelling
	Handwriting and presentation
	Standard English
	Language structure

Source: DfEE/QCA 1999a: 16–21

Note
* Bracketed statements relate to key stage 2 only.

General expectations for English in the primary school are that during key stage 1 pupils:

> learn to speak confidently and listen to what others have to say. They begin to read and write independently and with enthusiasm. They use language to explore their own experiences and imaginary worlds.
>
> DfEE/QCA 1999a: 16

while in key stage 2 they:

> learn to change the way they speak and write to suit different situations, purposes and audiences. They read a range of texts and respond to different layers of meaning in them. They explore the use of language in literary and non-literary texts and learn how language works.
>
> DfEE/QCA 1999a: 22

Behind each of the main headings in Table A1.1, i.e. 'speaking and listening', 'reading' and 'writing', are a whole series of statements detailing the specific knowledge and skills that teachers are required to teach over the period of the key stage.

Under 'speaking and listening', for example, we see in Table A1.1 six subheadings:

* speaking
* listening
* group discussion and interaction
* drama
* standard English
* language variation.

Within 'speaking' we find the following elaboration for key stage 1:

> To speak clearly, fluently and confidently to different people, pupils should be taught to:
>
> a speak with clear diction and appropriate intonation
> b choose words with precision
> c organise what they say
> d focus on the main point(s)
> e include relevant detail
> f take into account the needs of their listeners.
>
> DfEE/QCA 1999a: 16

and this information for key stage 2:

> To speak with confidence in a range of contexts, adapting their speech for a range of purposes and audiences, pupils should be taught to:
>
> a use vocabulary and syntax that enables them to communicate more complex meanings
> b gain and maintain the interest and response of different audiences
> c choose material that is relevant to the topic and to the listeners
> d show clear shape and organisation with an introduction and an ending

   e speak audibly and clearly, using spoken standard English in formal contexts
   f evaluate their speech and reflect on how it varies.

DfEE/QCA 1999a: 22

   For full details of the specific knowledge and skills that teachers are required to cover under each major and minor heading in Table A1.1 you should consult the complete curriculum document for English (DfEE/QCA 1999a).

   The detailed statements covering the knowledge, skills and understanding that pupils are expected to acquire during each key stage are accompanied by guidance on 'breadth of study'. This essentially overviews the range of materials that pupils are expected to be introduced to, and the types of activity they are expected to be involved in during their learning in each key stage, in different contexts and with different purposes. For 'speaking' during key stage 1, for example, the range of activity should include:

   a telling stories, real and imagined
   b reading aloud and reciting
   c describing events and experiences
   d speaking to different people, including friends, the class, teachers and other adults.

DfEE/QCA 1999a: 17

Mathematics

The mathematics programmes of study for key stages 1 and 2 (Table A1.2) both list all of the knowledge and skills that pupils should be taught under 'number' and 'shape, space and measures', with the key stage 2 programme also addressing requirements for 'handling data'; elements of 'handling data' are subsumed under 'number' at key stage 1, in preparation for later work in this area.

   In the mathematics programme of study for key stage 1 we read that:

Table A1.2 Skeletal outline of the key stage 1 and 2 programmes of study for mathematics*

Number	Using and applying number
	Numbers and the number system
	Calculations
	Solving numerical problems
	(Processing, representing and interpreting data)
Shape, space and measures	Using and applying shape, space and measures
	(Understanding patterns and properties of shape)
	Understanding properties of position and movement
	Understanding measures
Handling data (key stage 2 only)	Using and applying handling data
	Processing, representing and interpreting data

Source: DfEE/QCA 1999b: 16–21

Note
* Bracketed statements relate to key stage 1 only; 'handling data' features separately only at key stage 2.

During key stage 1 pupils develop their knowledge and understanding of mathematics through practical activity, exploration and discussion. They learn to count, read, write and order numbers to 100 and beyond. They develop a range of mental calculation skills and use these confidently in different settings. They learn about shape and space through practical activity which builds on their understanding of their immediate environment. They begin to grasp mathematical language, using it to talk about their methods and explain their reasoning when solving problems.

DfEE/QCA 1999b: 16

For key stage 2 we find the following multifaceted expectation:

During key stage 2 pupils use the number system more confidently. They move from counting reliably to calculating fluently with all four number operations. They always try to tackle a problem with mental methods before using any other approach. Pupils explore features of shape and space and develop their measuring skills in a range of contexts. They discuss and present their methods and reasoning using a wider range of mathematical language, diagrams and charts.

DfEE/QCA 1999b: 21

For a clear example of how the teaching expectations within each heading differ from one key stage to the other, reflecting learning progression, we can look at 'numbers and the number system' under 'number'. There are three topics under this heading at key stage 1: 'counting', 'number patterns and sequences' and 'the number system'. At key stage 2 there are five topics: 'counting', 'number patterns and sequences', 'integers', 'fractions, percentages and ratio' and 'decimals'. If we look specifically at 'counting' we find under key stage 1 that pupils should be taught to:

count reliably up to 20 objects at first and recognise that if the objects are rearranged the number stays the same; be familiar with the numbers 11 to 20; gradually extend counting to 100 and beyond.

DfEE/QCA 1999b: 16

while at key stage 2 they are to be taught to:

count on and back in tens or hundreds from any two- or three-digit number; recognise and continue number sequences formed by counting on or back in steps of constant size from any integer, extending to negative integers when counting back.

DfEE/QCA 1999b: 21

For a more complex example, we could look at 'using and applying number'. This has three subheadings at both stages: 'problem solving', 'communicating' and 'reasoning'. Under 'problem solving' at key stage 1 we find that pupils should be taught to:

a approach problems involving number, and data presented in a variety of forms, in order to identify what they need to do
b develop flexible approaches to problem solving and look for ways to overcome difficulties

c make decisions about which operations and problem-solving strategies to use

d organise and check their work

DfEE/QCA 1999b: 16

while during key stage 2 pupils should be taught to:

a make connections in mathematics and appreciate the need to use numerical skills and knowledge when solving problems in other parts of the mathematics curriculum

b break down a more complex problem or calculation into simpler steps before attempting a solution; identify the information needed to carry out the tasks

c select and use appropriate mathematical equipment, including ICT

d find different ways of approaching a problem in order to overcome any difficulties

e make mental estimates of the answers to calculations; check results.

DfEE/QCA 1999b: 21

Without analysing these statements in great detail it will be clear that they are less immediately interpretable than are those for 'counting'. This will have implications both for how schools and teachers set about delivering this aspect of the curriculum and in how they assess it internally.

As far as 'breadth of study' is concerned, at key stage 1 pupils should apparently be taught the 'knowledge, skills and understanding' through:

a practical activity, exploration and discussion

b using mathematical ideas in practical activities, then recording these using objects, pictures, diagrams, words, numbers and symbols

c using mental images of numbers and their relationships to support the development of mental calculation strategies

d estimating, drawing and measuring in a range of practical contexts

e drawing inferences from data in practical activities

f exploring and using a variety of resources and materials, including ICT

g activities that encourage them to make connections between number work and other aspects of their work in mathematics.

DfEE/QCA 1999b: 20

while at key stage 2 they should be involved in:

a activities that extend their understanding of the number system to include integers, fractions and decimals

b approximating and estimating more systematically in their work in mathematics

c using patterns and relationships to explore simple algebraic ideas

d applying their measuring skills in a range of contexts

e drawing inferences from data in practical activities, and recognising the difference between meaningful and misleading representations of data

f exploring and using a variety of resources and materials, including ICT

g activities in which pupils decide when the use of calculators is appropriate and then use them effectively

h using mathematics in their work in other subjects.

DfEE/QCA 1999b: 28

Science

Alongside the key stage 1 programme of study for science (outlined in Table A1.3) it is noted that during this key stage pupils:

> observe, explore and ask questions about living things, materials and phenomena. They begin to work together to collect evidence to help them answer questions and to link this to simple scientific ideas. They evaluate evidence and consider whether tests or comparisons are fair. They use reference materials to find out more about scientific ideas. They share their ideas and communicate them using scientific language, drawings, charts and tables.
>
> DfEE/QCA 1999c: 16

In the key stage 2 programme of study the statement is expanded and extended to reflect expected learning development:

> During key stage 2 pupils learn about a wider range of living things, materials and phenomena. They begin to make links between ideas and to explain things using simple models and theories. They apply their knowledge and understanding of scientific ideas to familiar phenomena, everyday things and their personal health. They begin to think about the positive and negative effects of scientific and technological developments on the environment and in other contexts. They carry out more systematic investigations, working on their own and with others. They use a range of reference sources in their work. They talk about their work and its significance, and communicate ideas using a wide range of scientific language, conventional diagrams, charts and graphs.
>
> DfEE/QCA 1999c: 21

Table A1.3 Skeletal outline of the key stage 1 and 2 programmes of study for science*

Scientific enquiry	Ideas and evidence in science
	Investigative skills
Life processes and living things	Life processes
	Humans and other animals
	Green plants
	Variation and classification
	Living things in their environment
Materials and their properties	Grouping (and classifying) materials
	Changing materials
	(Separating mixtures of materials)
Physical processes	Electricity
	Forces and motion
	Light and sound
	(The Earth and beyond)

Source: DfEE/QCA 1999c: 16–27

Note
* Bracketed statements relate to key stage 2 only.

Science learning, like learning in English and mathematics, and indeed in virtually any other school subject, is wide-ranging, as the statements of learning just quoted make clear. Through a variety of different types of activity, including whole class teaching, group projects, ICT-based work, practical investigations, and so on, pupils are expected to acquire a very broad range of knowledge, understanding and skills.

Here again it might be interesting to look at an example or two of how the specific statements under each topic heading in the programmes of study vary from one key stage to the other. Take, for instance, 'variation and classification' under 'life processes and living things'. At key stage 1 we find that pupils should be taught to:

a recognise similarities and differences between themselves and others, and to treat others with sensitivity
b group living things according to observable similarities and differences.

DfEE/QCA 1999c: 17

While at key stage 2 they should be taught:

a about environmental and inherited causes of variation within a species
b to classify living things into the major taxonomic groups
c that selective breeding can lead to new varieties.

DfEE/QCA 1999c: 31

Note the relevance of the minibeasts activity described in Chapter 2 to the key stage 1 teaching requirements, and how that simple sorting exercise and others like it should lead to the further learning referred to in the key stage 2 statements.

For a second example of intended learning development we can look at 'electricity' under 'physical processes'. At key stage 1 pupils should be taught:

a about everyday appliances that use electricity
b about simple series circuits involving batteries, wires, bulbs and other components
c how a switch can be used to break a circuit.

DfEE/QCA 1999c: 19

while by key stage 2 understanding of simple circuits is extended, with pupils required to be taught:

a to construct circuits, incorporating a battery or power supply and a range of switches, to make electrical devices work
b how changing the number or type of components in a series circuit can make bulbs brighter or dimmer
c how to represent series circuits by drawings and conventional symbols, and how to construct series circuits on the basis of drawings and diagrams using conventional symbols.

DfEE/QCA 1999c: 26

Again, note that schools have a great deal of flexibility in terms of when within the key stage they choose to teach any particular part of any particular topic, and teachers have flexibility as well in terms of how, and for how long, they teach them.

Under 'breadth of study' in science, the programme of study states that during both key stage 1 and key stage 2, pupils should be taught the relevant knowledge, skills and understanding through:

a a range of domestic and environmental contexts that are familiar and of interest to them
b looking at the part science has played in the development of many useful things
c using a range of sources of information and data, including ICT-based sources
d using first-hand and secondary data to carry out a range of scientific investigations, including complete investigations.

DfEE/QCA 1999c: 20, 27

In science, 'breadth of study' extends further to cover 'communication' and 'health and safety'. Under 'communication' key stage 1 pupils should be taught to 'use simple scientific language to communicate ideas and to name and describe living things, materials, phenomena and processes', which develops for key stage 2 into 'use appropriate scientific language and terms, including SI units of measurement [for example, metre, newton], to communicate ideas and explain the behaviour of living things, materials, phenomena and processes'. Under 'health and safety' pupils in both key stages are to be taught to 'recognise that there are hazards in living things, materials and physical processes, and assess risks and take action to reduce risks to themselves and others' (DfEE/QCA 1999c: 20, 27).

National Curriculum attainment targets

English, mathematics and science

The tables in this appendix reproduce the level descriptions for levels 1 to 5 only, for each attainment target in the three core subjects as they applied in 2011. These are the levels most relevant for primary teachers who are required to provide level judgements for their pupils at the end of key stage 1 and at the end of key stage 2. At the end of key stage 1 (age seven) most pupils are expected to have reached level 2 in each attainment target in each subject; at the end of key stage 2 (age eleven) most pupils are expected to have reached level 4.

For the full set of level descriptions you should consult the relevant curriculum documents: DfEE/QCA 1999a (English), 1999b (Mathematics), 1999c (Science).

Table A2.1 English – speaking and listening (En1): levels 1 to 5

Level 1

Pupils talk about matters of immediate interest. They listen to others and usually respond appropriately. They convey simple meanings to a range of listeners, speaking audibly, and begin to extend their ideas or accounts by providing some detail.

Level 2

Pupils begin to show confidence in talking and listening, particularly where the topics interest them. On occasions, they show awareness of the needs of the listener by including relevant detail. In developing and explaining their ideas they speak clearly and use a growing vocabulary. They usually listen carefully and respond with increasing appropriateness to what others say. They are beginning to be aware that in some situations a more formal vocabulary and tone of voice are used.

Level 3

Pupils talk and listen confidently in different contexts, exploring and communicating ideas. In discussion, they show understanding of the main points. Through relevant comments and questions, they show they have listened carefully. They begin to adapt what they say to the needs of the listener, varying the use of vocabulary and the level of detail. They are beginning to be aware of standard English and when it is used.

Level 4

Pupils talk and listen with confidence in an increasing range of contexts. Their talk is adapted to the purpose: developing ideas thoughtfully, describing events and conveying their opinions clearly. In discussion, they listen carefully, making contributions and asking questions that are responsive to others' ideas and views. They use appropriately some of the features of standard English vocabulary and grammar.

Level 5

Pupils talk and listen confidently in a wide range of contexts, including some that are of a formal nature. Their talk engages the interest of the listener as they begin to vary their expression and vocabulary. In discussion, they pay close attention to what others say, ask questions to develop ideas and make contributions that take account of others' views. They begin to use standard English in formal situations.

Source: DfEE/QCA 1999a: 55–6

Table A2.2 English – reading (En2): levels 1 to 5

Level 1
Pupils recognise familiar words in simple texts. They use their knowledge of letters and sound–symbol relationships in order to read words and to establish meaning when reading aloud. In these activities they sometimes require support. They express their response to poems, stories and non-fiction by identifying aspects they like.

Level 2
Pupils' reading of simple texts shows understanding and is generally accurate. They express opinions about major events or ideas in stories, poems and non-fiction. They use more than one strategy, such as phonic, graphic, syntactic and contextual, in reading unfamiliar words and establishing meaning.

Level 3
Pupils read a range of texts fluently and accurately. They read independently, using strategies appropriately to establish meaning. In responding to fiction and non-fiction they show understanding of the main points and express preferences. They use their knowledge of the alphabet to locate books and find information.

Level 4
In responding to a range of texts, pupils show understanding of significant ideas, themes, events and characters, beginning to use inference and deduction. They refer to the text when explaining their views. They locate and use ideas and information.

Level 5
Pupils show understanding of a range of texts, selecting essential points and using inference and deduction where appropriate. In their responses, they identify key features, themes and characters and select sentences, phrases and relevant information to support their views. They retrieve and collate information from a range of sources.

Source: DfEE/QCA 1999a: 57–8

Table A2.3 English – writing (En3): levels 1 to 5

Level 1

Pupils' writing communicates meaning through simple words and phrases. In their reading or their writing, pupils begin to show awareness of how full stops are used. Letters are usually clearly shaped and correctly orientated.

Level 2

Pupils' writing communicates meaning in both narrative and non-narrative forms, using appropriate and interesting vocabulary, and showing some awareness of the reader. Ideas are developed in a sequence of sentences, sometimes demarcated by capital letters and full stops. Simple, monosyllabic words are usually spelt correctly, and where there are inaccuracies the alternative is phonetically plausible. In handwriting, letters are accurately formed and consistent in size.

Level 3

Pupils' writing is often organised, imaginative and clear. The main features of different forms of writing are used appropriately, beginning to be adapted to different readers. Sequences of sentences extend ideas logically and words are chosen for variety and interest. The basic grammatical structure of sentences is usually correct. Spelling is usually accurate, including that of common, polysyllabic words. Punctuation to mark sentences – full stops, capital letters and question marks – is used accurately. Handwriting is joined and legible.

Level 4

Pupils' writing in a range of forms is lively and thoughtful. Ideas are often sustained and developed in interesting ways and organised appropriately for the purpose of the reader. Vocabulary choices are often adventurous and words are used for effect. Pupils are beginning to use grammatically complex sentences, extending meaning. Spelling, including that of polysyllabic words that conform to regular patterns, is generally accurate. Full stops, capital letters and question marks are used correctly, and pupils are beginning to use punctuation within the sentence. Handwriting style is fluent, joined and legible.

Level 5

Pupils' writing is varied and interesting, conveying meaning clearly in a range of forms for different readers, using a more formal style where appropriate. Vocabulary choices are imaginative and words are used precisely. Simple and complex sentences are organised into paragraphs. Words with complex regular patterns are usually spelt correctly. A range of punctuation, including commas, apostrophes and inverted commas, is usually used accurately. Handwriting is joined, clear and fluent and, where appropriate, is adapted to a range of tasks.

Source: DfEE/QCA 1999a: 59–60

Table A2.4 Mathematics – using and applying mathematics (Ma1): levels 1 to 5

Level 1

Pupils use mathematics as an integral part of classroom activities. They represent their work with objects or pictures and discuss it. They recognise and use a simple pattern or relationship.

Level 2

Pupils select the mathematics they use in some classroom activities. They discuss their work using mathematical language and are beginning to represent it using symbols and simple diagrams. They explain why an answer is correct.

Level 3

Pupils try different approaches and find ways of overcoming difficulties that arise when they are solving problems. They are beginning to organise their work and check results. Pupils discuss their mathematical work and are beginning to explain their thinking. They use and interpret mathematical symbols and diagrams. Pupils show that they understand a general statement by finding particular examples that match it.

Level 4

Pupils develop their own strategies for solving problems and use these strategies both in working within mathematics and in applying mathematics to practical contexts. When solving problems, with or without ICT, they check their results are reasonable by considering the context. They look for patterns and relationships, presenting information and results in a clear and organised way, using ICT appropriately. They search for a solution by trying out ideas of their own.

Level 5

In order to explore mathematical situations, carry out tasks or tackle problems, pupils identify the mathematical aspects and obtain necessary information. They calculate accurately, using ICT where appropriate. They check their working and results, considering whether these are sensible. They show understanding of situations by describing them mathematically using symbols, words and diagrams. They draw simple conclusions of their own and explain their reasoning.

Source: DfEE/QCA 1999b: 87–8

Table A2.5 Mathematics – number (Ma2): levels 1 to 5

Level 1

Pupils count, order, add and subtract numbers when solving problems in practical contexts. They read and write the numbers involved.

Level 2

Pupils count sets of objects reliably, and use mental recall of addition and subtraction facts to 10. They begin to understand the place value of each digit in a number and use this to order numbers up to 100. They choose the appropriate operation when solving addition and subtraction problems. They use the knowledge that subtraction is the inverse of addition. They use mental calculation strategies to solve number problems involving money and measures. They recognise sequences of numbers, including odd and even numbers.

Level 3

Pupils show understanding of place value in numbers up to 1000 and use this to make approximations. They begin to use decimal notation, in the context of measures and money, and to recognise negative numbers in practical contexts such as temperature. Pupils use mental recall of addition and subtraction facts to 20 in solving problems involving larger numbers. They add and subtract numbers with two digits mentally and numbers with three digits using written methods. They use mental recall of the 2, 3, 4, 5 and 10 multiplication tables and derive the associated division facts. They solve whole-number problems involving multiplication or division, including those that give rise to remainders. They use simple fractions that are several parts of a whole and recognise when two simple fractions are equivalent.

Level 4

Pupils use their understanding of place value to mentally multiply and divide whole numbers by 10 or 100. When solving number problems, they use a range of mental methods of computation with the four operations, including mental recall of multiplication facts up to 10 × 10 and quick derivation of corresponding division facts. They select efficient strategies for addition, subtraction, multiplication and division. They recognise approximate proportions of a whole and use simple fractions and percentages to describe these. They begin to use simple formulae expressed in words.

Level 5

Pupils use their understanding of place value to multiply and divide whole numbers and decimals. They order, add and subtract negative numbers in context. They use all four operations with decimals to two places. They solve simple problems involving ratio and direct proportion. They calculate fractional or percentage parts of quantities and measurements, using a calculator where appropriate. They construct, express in symbolic form and use simple formulae involving one or two operations. They use brackets appropriately. They use and interpret coordinates in all four quadrants.

Source: DfEE/QCA 1999b: 89–90

Table A2.6 Mathematics – shape, space and measures (Ma3): levels 1 to 5

Level 1
When working with 2-D and 3-D shapes, pupils use mathematical language to describe properties and positions. They measure and order objects using direct comparison, and order events.

Level 2
Pupils use mathematical names for common 3-D and 2-D shapes and describe their properties, including numbers of sides and corners. They distinguish between straight and turning movements, understand angle as a measurement of turn, and recognise right angles in turns. They begin to use everyday non-standard and standard units to measure length and mass.

Level 3
Pupils classify 3-D and 2-D shapes in various ways using mathematical properties such as reflective symmetry for 2-D shapes. They use non-standard units, standard metric units of length, capacity and mass, and standard units of time, in a range of contexts.

Level 4
Pupils make 3-D mathematical models by linking given faces or edges, draw common 2-D shapes in different orientations on grids. They reflect simple shapes in a mirror line. They choose and use appropriate units and instruments, interpreting, with appropriate accuracy, numbers on a range of measuring instruments. They find perimeters of simple shapes and find areas by counting squares.

Level 5
When constructing models and when drawing or using shapes, pupils measure and draw angles to the nearest degree, and use language associated with angle. Pupils know the angle sum of a triangle and that of angles at a point. They identify all the symmetries of 2-D shapes. They know the rough metric equivalents of imperial units still in daily use and convert one metric unit to another. They make sensible estimates of a range of measures in relation to everyday situations. Pupils understand and use the formula for the area of a rectangle.

Source: DfEE/QCA 1999b: 91–2

Table A2.7 Mathematics – handling data* (Ma4): levels 1 to 5

Level 1
Pupils sort objects and classify them, demonstrating the criterion they have used.

Level 2
Pupils sort objects and classify them using more than one criterion. When they have gathered information, pupils record results in simple lists, tables and block graphs, in order to communicate their findings.

Level 3
Pupils extract and interpret information presented in simple tables and lists. They construct bar charts and pictograms, where the symbol represents a group of units, to communicate information they have gathered, and they interpret information presented to them in these forms.

Level 4
Pupils collect discrete data and record them using a frequency table. They understand and use the mode and range to describe sets of data. They group data, where appropriate, in equal class intervals, represent collected data in frequency diagrams and interpret such diagrams. They construct and interpret simple line graphs.

Level 5
Pupils understand and use the mean of discrete data. They compare two simple distributions, using the range and one of the mode, median or mean. They interpret graphs and diagrams, including pie charts, and draw conclusions. They understand and use the probability scale from 0 to 1. Pupils find and justify probabilities, and approximations to these, by selecting and using methods based on equally likely outcomes and experimental evidence, as appropriate. They understand that different outcomes may result from repeating an experiment.

Source: DfEE/QCA 1999b: 93–4

Note
*   This attainment target applies to key stage 2 only.

Table A2.8 Science – scientific enquiry* (Sc1): levels 1 to 5

Level 1

Pupils describe or respond appropriately to simple features of objects, living things and events they observe, communicating their findings in simple ways [for example, talking about their work, through drawings, simple charts].

Level 2

Pupils respond to suggestions about how to find things out and, with help, make their own suggestions about how to collect data to answer questions. They use simple texts, with help, to find information. They use simple equipment provided and make observations related to their task. They observe and compare objects, living things and events. They describe their observations using scientific vocabulary and record them, using simple tables when appropriate. They say whether what happened was what they expected.

Level 3

Pupils respond to suggestions and put forward their own ideas about how to find the answer to a question. They recognise why it is important to collect data to answer questions. They use simple texts to find information. They make relevant observations and measure quantities, such as length or mass, using a range of simple equipment. Where appropriate, they carry out a fair test with some help, recognising and explaining why it is fair. They record their observations in a variety of ways. They provide explanations for observations and for simple patterns in recorded measurements. They communicate in a scientific way what they have found out and suggest improvements in their work.

Level 4

Pupils recognise that scientific ideas are based on evidence. In their own investigative work, they decide on an appropriate approach [for example, using a fair test] to answer a question. Where appropriate, they describe, or show in the way they perform their task, how to vary one factor while keeping others the same. Where appropriate, they make predictions. They select information from sources provided for them. They select suitable equipment and make a series of observations and measurements that are adequate for the task. They record their observations, comparisons and measurements using tables and bar charts. They begin to plot points to form simple graphs, and use these graphs to point out and interpret patterns in their data. They begin to relate their conclusions to these patterns and to scientific knowledge and understanding, and to communicate them with appropriate scientific language. They suggest improvements in their work, giving reasons.

Level 5

Pupils describe how experimental evidence and creative thinking have been combined to provide a scientific explanation [for example, Jenner's work on vaccination at key stage 2, Lavoisier's work on burning at key stage 3]. When they try to answer a scientific question, they identify an appropriate approach. They select from a range of sources of information. When the investigation involves a fair test, they identify key factors to be considered. Where appropriate, they make predictions based on their scientific knowledge and understanding. They select apparatus for a range of tasks and plan to use it effectively. They make a series of observations, comparisons or measurements with precision appropriate to the task. They begin to repeat observations and measurements and to offer simple explanations for any differences they encounter. They record observations and measurements systematically and, where appropriate, present data as line graphs. They draw conclusions that are consistent with the evidence and begin to relate these to scientific knowledge and understanding. They make practical suggestions about how their working methods could be improved. They use appropriate scientific language and conventions to communicate quantitative and qualitative data.

Source: DfEE/QCA 1999c: 75

Note
* Bracketed examples are not statutory.

Table A2.9 Science – life processes and living things* (Sc2): levels 1 to 5

Level 1
Pupils recognise and name external parts of the body [for example, head, arm] and of plants [for example, leaf, flower]. They communicate observations of a range of animals and plants in terms of features [for example, colour of coat, size of leaf]. They recognise and identify a range of common animals [for example, fly, goldfish, robin].

Level 2
Pupils use their knowledge about living things to describe the basic conditions [for example, a supply of food, water, air, light] that animals and plants need in order to survive. They recognise that living things grow and reproduce. They sort living things into groups, using simple features. They describe the basis for their groupings [for example, number of legs, shape of leaf]. They recognise that different living things are found in different places [for example, ponds, woods].

Level 3
Pupils use their knowledge and understanding of basic life processes [for example, growth, reproduction] when they describe differences between living and non-living things. They provide simple explanations for changes in living things [for example, diet affecting the health of humans or other animals, lack of light or water altering plant growth]. They identify ways in which an animal is suited to its environment [for example, a fish having fins to help it swim].

Level 4
Pupils demonstrate knowledge and understanding of life processes and living things drawn from the key stage 2 or key stage 3 programme of study. They use scientific names for some major organs of body systems [for example, the heart at key stage 2, the stomach at key stage 3] and identify the position of these organs in the human body. They identify organs [for example, stamen at key stage 2, stigma, root hairs at key stage 3] of different plants they observe. They use keys based on observable external features to help them to identify and group living things systematically. They recognise that feeding relationships exist between plants and animals in a habitat, and describe these relationships using food chains and terms [for example, predator and prey].

Level 5
Pupils demonstrate an increasing knowledge and understanding of life processes and living things drawn from the key stage 2 or key stage 3 programme of study. They describe the main functions of organs of the human body [for example, the heart at key stage 2, stomach at key stage 3], and of the plant [for example, the stamen at key stage 2, root hairs at key stage 3]. They explain how these functions are essential to the organism. They describe the main stages of the life cycles of humans and flowering plants and point out similarities. They recognise that there is a great variety of living things and understand the importance of classification. They explain that different organisms are found in different habitats because of differences in environmental factors [for example, the availability of light or water].

Source: DfEE/QCA 1999c: 77–8

Note
*   Bracketed examples are not statutory.

Table A2.10 Science – materials and their properties* (Sc3): levels 1 to 5

Level 1
Pupils know about a range of properties [for example, texture, appearance] and communicate observations of materials in terms of these properties.

Level 2
Pupils identify a range of common materials and know about some of their properties. They describe similarities and differences between materials. They sort materials into groups and describe the basis for their groupings in everyday terms [for example, shininess, hardness, smoothness]. They describe ways in which some materials are changed by heating or cooling or by processes such as bending or stretching.

Level 3
Pupils use their knowledge and understanding of materials when they describe a variety of ways of sorting them into groups according to their properties. They explain simply why some materials are particularly suitable for specific purposes [for example, glass for windows, copper for electrical cables]. They recognise that some changes [for example, the freezing of water] can be reversed and some [for example, the baking of clay] cannot, and they classify changes in this way.

Level 4
Pupils demonstrate knowledge and understanding of materials and their properties drawn from the key stage 2 or key stage 3 programme of study. They describe differences between the properties of different materials and explain how these differences are used to classify substances [for example, as solids, liquids, gases at key stage 2, as acids, alkalis at key stage 3]. They describe some methods [for example, filtration, distillation] that are used to separate simple mixtures. They use scientific terms [for example, evaporation, condensation] to describe changes. They use knowledge about some reversible and irreversible changes to make simple predictions about whether other changes are reversible or not.

Level 5
Pupils demonstrate an increasing knowledge and understanding of materials and their properties drawn from the key stage 2 or key stage 3 programme of study. They describe some metallic properties [for example, good electrical conductivity] and use these properties to distinguish metals from other solids. They identify a range of contexts in which changes [for example, evaporation, condensation] take place. They use knowledge about how a specific mixture [for example, salt and water, sand and water] can be separated to suggest ways in which other similar mixtures might be separated.

Source: DfEE/QCA 1999c: 79–80

Note
* Bracketed examples are not statutory.

Table A2.11 Science – physical processes* (Sc4): levels 1 to 5

Level 1

Pupils communicate observations of changes in light, sound or movement that result from actions [for example, switching on a simple electrical circuit, pushing and pulling objects]. They recognise that sound and light come from a variety of sources and name some of these.

Level 2

Pupils know about a range of physical phenomena and recognise and describe similarities and differences associated with them. They compare the way in which devices [for example, bulbs] work in different electrical circuits. They compare the brightness or colour of lights, and the loudness or pitch of sounds. They compare the movement of different objects in terms of speed or direction.

Level 3

Pupils use their knowledge and understanding of physical phenomena to link cause and effect in simple explanations [for example, a bulb failing to light because of a break in an electrical circuit, the direction or speed of movement of an object changing because of a push or a pull]. They begin to make simple generalisations about physical phenomena [for example, explaining that sounds they hear become fainter the further they are from the source].

Level 4

Pupils demonstrate knowledge and understanding of physical processes drawn from the key stage 2 or key stage 3 programme of study. They describe and explain physical phenomena [for example, how a particular device may be connected to work in an electrical circuit, how the apparent position of the Sun changes over the course of a day]. They make generalisations about physical phenomena [for example, motion is affected by forces, including gravitational attraction, magnetic attraction and friction]. They use physical ideas to explain simple phenomena [for example, the formation of shadows, sounds being heard through a variety of materials].

Level 5

Pupils demonstrate knowledge and understanding of physical processes drawn from the key stage 2 or key stage 3 programme of study. They use ideas to explain how to make a range of changes [for example, altering the current in a circuit, altering the pitch or loudness of a sound]. They use some abstract ideas in descriptions of familiar phenomena [for example, objects are seen when light from them enters the eye at key stage 2, forces are balanced when an object is stationary at key stage 3]. They use simple models to explain effects that are caused by the movement of the Earth [for example, the length of a day or year].

Source: DfEE/QCA 1999c: 81–2

Note
* Bracketed examples are not statutory.

References

AAP (2005a) *Sixth Survey of Science 2003*, an Assessment of Achievement Programme report, Edinburgh: Scottish Executive Education Department.

AAP (2005b) *Seventh Survey of Mathematics 2004*, an Assessment of Achievement Programme report, Edinburgh: Scottish Executive Education Department.

Anderson, L.W. (ed.), Krathwohl, D.R. (ed), Airasian, P.W., Cruikshank, K.A., Mayer, R.E., Pintrich, P.R., Raths, J. and Wittrock, M.C. (2001) *A Taxonomy for Learning, Teaching and Assessing: A Revision of Bloom's Taxonomy of Educational Objectives,* New York: Longman.

APU (1979) *Science Progress Report 1977–78,* London: Assessment of Performance Unit.

Archenhold, F., Bell, J., Donnelly, J., Johnson, S. and Welford, G. (1988) *Science at Age 15. A Review of APU Survey Findings 1980–84,* London: HMSO.

ARG (1999) *Assessment for Learning: Beyond the Black Box.* University of Cambridge: Assessment Reform Group.

ARG (2002a) *Assessment for Learning: 10 Principles.* University of Cambridge: Assessment Reform Group.

ARG (2002b) *Testing, Motivation and Learning.* University of Cambridge: Assessment Reform Group.

ARG (undated) *The Role of Teachers in the Assessment of Learning.* London: Institute of Education.

Bew (2011) *Independent Review of Key Stage 2 testing, assessment and accountability,* Final Report to the British Government Department for Education.

Black, P. (1998) 'Learning, League tables and National Assessment: opportunity lost or hope deferred?', *Oxford Review of Education,* 24: 57–68.

Black, P and Wiliam, D. (1998a) *Inside the Black Box,* London: King's College School of Education.

Black, P and Wiliam, D. (1998b) 'Assessment and classroom learning', *Assessment in Education,* 5: 7–74.

Black, P., Harrison, C., Lee, C., Marshall, B. and Wiliam, D. (2002) *Working Inside the Black Box,* London: King's College Department of Education and Professional Studies.

Black, P., Harrison, C., Lee, C., Marshall, B. and Wiliam, D. (2003) *Assessment for Learning: Putting it into Practice,* Maidenhead: Open University Press.

Bloom, B. S. (ed.), Engelhart, M.D., Furst, E.J., Hill, W.H. and Krathwohl, D.R. (1956) *Taxonomy of Educational Objectives: The Classification of Educational Goals. Handbook 1: Cognitive Domain,* New York: David McKay.

Bradshaw, J., Ager, R., Burge, B. and Wheater, R. (2010a). *PISA 2009: Achievements of 15-year-olds in England.* Slough: NFER.

Bradshaw, J., Ager, R., Burge, B. and Wheater, R. (2010b). *PISA 2009: Achievements of 15-year-olds in Northern Ireland.* Slough: NFER.

Bradshaw, J., Ager, R., Burge, B. and Wheater, R. (2010c). *PISA 2009: Achievements of 15-year-olds in Wales.* Slough: NFER.

Bradshaw, J., Sturman, L., Vappula, H., Ager, R. and Wheater, R. (2007a). *Achievement of 15-year-olds in England: PISA 2006 National Report.* Slough: NFER.

Bradshaw, J., Sturman, L., Vappula, H., Ager, R. and Wheater, R. (2007b). *Achievement of 15-year-olds in Wales: PISA 2006 National Report.* Slough: NFER.

Bramley, T. (2006) *Equating Methods Used in KS3 Science and English,* Cambridge: Cambridge Assessment.

Brook, A., Briggs, H., Bell, B. and Driver, R. (1984) *Aspects of Secondary Students' Understanding of Heat: Summary Report,* Leeds: University of Leeds Centre for Studies in Science and Mathematics Education.

Brown, M., Taggart, B., McCallum, B. and Gipps, C. (1996) 'The impact of key stage 2 tests', *Education 3 to 13,* 24: 3–7.

Burgess, S. and Greaves, E. (2009) *Test Scores, Subjective Assessment and Stereotyping of Ethnic Minorities,* Working paper 09/221, Bristol: University of Bristol Centre for Market and Public Organization.

Cale, A. and Burr, K. (2007) *Foundation Stage Profile Moderation 2006–07,* Surrey County Council.

Campbell, J.R., Kelly, D.L., Mullis, I.V.S., Martin, M.O. and Sainsbury, M. (2001) *Framework and Specifications for PIRLS Assessment 2001,* 2nd edition, Chestnut Hill, MA: Boston College.

Clarke, C. (1997) 'The impact of national curriculum statutory testing at key stages 1 and 2 on teaching and learning and the curriculum', *British Journal of Curriculum and Assessment,* 7: 12–18.

Clarke, S. (2001) *Unlocking Formative Assessment,* London: Hodder and Stoughton.

Clarke, S. (2005) *Formative Assessment in Action: Weaving the Elements Together,* London: Hodder and Stoughton.

Clarke, S. (2008) *Active Learning through Formative Assessment,* London: Hodder and Stoughton.

Clarke, S. and Gipps, C. (1998) 'The Role of teachers in teacher assessment in England 1996–1998', *Evaluation and Research in Education,* 14: 38–52.

Coldwell, M., Shipton, L., Stevens, A., Stiell, B., Willis, B. and Wolstenholme, C. (2011) *Process evaluation of the Year 1 Phonics Screening Check Pilot,* Research Brief DFE-RB159, London: Department for Education.

Comber, L.C. and Keeves, J.P. (1973) *Science Education in Nineteen Countries. International Studies in Evaluation I,* Uppsala: Almquist &Wiksell.

Condie, R., Robertson, I.J. and Napuk, A. (2003) 'The Assessment of Achievement Programme', in T.G.K. Bryce and W.M. Humes (eds), *Scottish Education,* Edinburgh: Edinburgh University Press.

Cowie, B. and Bell, B. (1999) 'A model of formative assessment in science education', *Assessment in Education,* 6: 101–17.

Cox, H. (2008) 'The developmental process for the optional teacher assessment materials for English for use in Wales at the end of key stage 2', *Education 3–13,* 36: 313–23.

Cresswell, M. (1994) 'Aggregation and awarding methods for national curriculum assessments in England and Wales', *Assessment in Education,* 1: 45–61.

Crocker, L. and Algina, J. (2006) *Introduction to Classical and Modern Test Theory,* Belmont CA: Wadsworth Group.

Crooks, T.J., Kane, M.T. and Cohen, A.S. (1996) 'Threats to the valid use of assessments', *Assessment in Education,* 3: 265–86.

Daugherty, R. (1995) *National Curriculum Assessment,* London: The Falmer Press.

Daugherty, R. (2004) *Learning Pathways Through Statutory Assessment: Key Stages 2 and 3,* Final Report submitted to the Welsh Assembly Government.

Daugherty, R. (2009) 'National curriculum assessment in Wales: adaptations and divergence', *Educational Research,* 51: 247–50.

DCELLS (2008a) *Framework for Children's Learning for 3 to 7-year-olds in Wales,* Cardiff: Department for Children, Education, Lifelong Learning and Skills.

DCELLS (2008b) *English in the National Curriculum for Wales Key Stages 2–4,* Cardiff: Department for Children, Education, Lifelong Learning and Skills.

DCELLS (2008c) *Welsh in the National Curriculum for Wales Key Stages 2–4,* Cardiff: Department for Children, Education, Lifelong Learning and Skills.

DCELLS (2008d) *Mathematics in the National Curriculum for Wales Key Stages 2–4*, Cardiff: Department for Children, Education, Lifelong Learning and Skills.

DCELLS (2008e) *Science in the National Curriculum for Wales Key Stages 2-4*, Cardiff: Department for Children, Education, Lifelong Learning and Skills.

DCELLS (2008f) *Ensuring Consistency in Teacher Assessment*, Cardiff: Department for Children, Education, Lifelong Learning and Skills.

DCELLS (2009a) *Statutory Assessment Arrangements for the School Year 2009/10,* Cardiff: Department for Children, Education, Lifelong Learning and Skills.

DCELLS (2009b) *Foundation Phase Child Development Profile Guidance*, Cardiff: Department for Children, Education, Lifelong Learning and Skills.

Dearing, R. (1993) *The National Curriculum and its Assessment: Final Report,* London: School Curriculum and Assessment Authority.

DENI (2007) *The Education (Assessment Arrangements) (Foundation to Key Stage 3) Order* (Northern Ireland) 2007, London: HMSO.

DENI (2010) InCAS. Circular Number: 2010/20. Dublin: Northern Ireland Department of Education.

DES (1966) *Progress in Reading 1948–1964,* a Department of Education and Science publication, London: HMSO.

DES (1975) *A Language for Life,* The Bullock Report, a Department of Education and Science publication, London: HMSO.

DES (1978) *Primary Education in England,* a Department of Education and Science publication, London: HMSO.

DfE (2010a) *Early Years Foundation Stage Profile Results in England 2009/10*, SFR 28/2010, London: Department for Education.

DfE (2010b) *National Curriculum Assessments at Key Stage 1 in England 2010,* Statistical First Release SFR 26/2010, London: Department for Education.

DfE (2010c) *Evaluation of the Single Level Test (SLT) Pilot Final Report*, London: Department for Education.

DfE (2010d) *National Curriculum Assessments at Key Stage 2 in England 2010 (revised)*, SFR 36/2010, London: Department for Education.

DfE (2010e) *Key Stage 2 Attainment of Pupils in Science in England, 2009/10,* Statistical First Release SFR 24/2010, London: Department for Education.

DfE (2011) *Response to Public Consultation on the Year 1 Phonics Screening Check*, London: Department for Education.

DfEE/QCA (1999a) *The National Curriculum for England: English Key Stages 1–4*, London: Department for Education and Employment and Qualifications and Curriculum Authority.

DfEE/QCA (1999b) *The National Curriculum for England: Mathematics Key Stages 1–4*, London: Department for Education and Employment and Qualifications and Curriculum Authority.

DfEE/QCA (1999c) *The National Curriculum for England: Science Key Stages 1–4*, London: Department for Education and Employment and Qualifications and Curriculum Authority.

DfES (2007). *Gender and Education: The Evidence on Pupils in England.* London: Department for Education and Skills.

Elwood, J. (2009) 'The English national curriculum assessment system: A commentary from Northern Ireland', *Educational Research*, 51:251–54.

Estyn (2010) *Evaluation of the arrangements to assure the consistency of teacher assessment in the core subjects at key stage 2 and key stage 3*, Cardiff: Her Majesty's Inspectorate for Education and Training in Wales.

Expert Group on Assessment (2009) *Report of the Expert Group on Assessment,* London: Department of Children, Schools and Families.

Foxman, D., Ruddock, G., Joffe, L., Mason, K., Mitchell, P. and Sexton, B. (1985) *A Review of Monitoring in Mathematics 1978 to 1982*, an Assessment of Performance Unit report, London: Department of Education and Science.

Foxman, D., Ruddock, G. and McCallum, I. (1990) *APU Mathematics Monitoring 1984–88 (Phase 2). A Summary of Findings*, Assessment Matters No.3, London: HMSO.

Foxman, D., Hutchison, D. and Bloomfield, B. (1991) *The APU Experience 1977–1990*, London: Schools Examination and Assessment Council.

Gardner, J. (ed.) (2006) *Assessment and Learning*, London: Sage.

Gardner, J., Harlen, W., Hayward, L. and Stobart, G. with Montgomery, M. (2010) *Developing Teacher Assessment*, Maidenhead: Open University Press.

Gill, B., Dunn, M. and Goddard, E. (2002). *Student Achievement in England: Results in Reading, Mathematical and Scientific Literacy Among 15-Year-olds from OECD PISA 2000 Study*, London: The Stationery Office.

Gorman, T. (1987) *Pupils' Attitudes to Reading*, an Assessment of Performance Unit report, Slough: NFER-Nelson.

Gorman, T. and Kispal, A. (1987) *The Assessment of Reading*, Slough: NFER-Nelson.

Gorman, T., White, J., Hargreaves, M., MacLure, M. and Tate, A. (1984) *Language Performance in Schools. 1982 Primary Survey Report*, an Assessment of Performance Unit publication, London: Department of Education and Science.

Gorman, T.P., White, J., Brooks, G., MacLure, M. and Kispal, A. (1988) *Language Performance in Schools. Review of APU Language Monitoring 1979–1983*, London: HMSO.

Hambleton, R.K., Swaminathan, H. and Rogers, H.J. (1991) *Fundamentals of Item Response Theory*, London: Sage Publications.

Harlen, W. (1983) *Science at Age 11,* an Assessment of Performance Unit report, London: Department of Education and Science.

Harlen, W. (1984) 'The Individual Practical Tasks', in Harlen, W., Black, P., Johnson, S., Palacio, D. and Russell, T., *Science in Schools. Age 11: Report no.3*, an Assessment of Performance Unit report, London: Department of Education and Science.

Harlen, W. (1988) 'The Performance of Investigations', in T. Russell (ed.) *Science at Age 11. A Review of APU Survey Findings 1980–84*, London: HMSO.

Harlen, W. (2004) *A Systematic Review of the Evidence of the Reliability and Validity of Assessment by Teachers for Summative Purposes*, London: EPPI-Centre.

Harlen, W. (2005) 'Trusting teachers' judgements: research evidence of the reliability and validity of teachers' assessment used for summative purposes', *Research Papers in Education*, 20: 245–70.

Harlen, W. (2006) 'On the Relationship between Assessment for Formative and Summative Purposes', in J. Gardner (ed.), *Assessment and Learning*, 103–18, London: Sage.

Harlen, W. (2007) *Assessment of Learning,* London: Sage.

Harmon, M., Smith, T. A., Martin, M. O., Kelly, D. L., Beaton, A. E., Mullis, I. V. S., Gonzales, E. J. and Orpwood, G. (1997) *Performance Assessment in IEA's Third International Mathematics and Science Study (TIMSS),* Chestnut Hill, MA: TIMSS International Study Centre, Boston College.

Hilton, M. (2006) 'Measuring standards in primary English: issues of validity and accountability with respect to PIRLS and National Curriculum test scores', *British Educational Research Journal*, 32: 817–37.

Horne, J., Bejtka, K. and Miller, S. (2008) *Trends in International Maths and Science Survey (TIMSS)) 2007 – Highlights from Scotland's Results,* Edinburgh: The Scottish Government.

Husen, T. and Postlethwaite, T.N. (1996) 'A brief history of the International Association for the Evaluation of Educational Achievement (IEA)', *Assessment in Education,* 3: 129–42.

Isaacs, T. (2010) 'Educational assessment in England', *Assessment in Education*, 17 (3): 315–34.

Johnson, S. (1989) *Monitoring Science Performance: The APU Experience*, London: HMSO.

Johnson, S. (1999) 'IEA science assessment in developing countries', *Assessment in Education,* 6: 57–74.

Johnson, S. (2011) *A Focus on Teacher Assessment Reliability in GCSE and GCE*, Coventry: Ofqual.

Johnson, S. and Munro, L. (2008) Teacher Judgements and Test Results: Should Teachers and Tests Agree? Paper presented at the Annual Conference of the Association of Educational Assessment – Europe.

Johnson, S. and Murphy, P. (1986) *Girls and Physics: Reflections on APU Survey Findings*, an Assessment of Performance Unit Occasional Paper, London: Department of Education and Science.

Keys, W., Harris, S. and Fernandes, C. (1996a) *Third International Maths and Science Study. First National Report Part 1,* Slough: NFER.

Keys, W., Harris, S. and Fernandes, C. (1996b) *Third International Maths and Science Study. National Reports Appendices,* Slough: NFER.

Krathwohl, D.R. (2002) 'A revision of Bloom's taxonomy: an Overview', *Theory into Practice*, 41: 212–18.

Krathwohl, D.R., Bloom, B.S. and Masia, B.B. (1964) *Taxonomy of Educational Objectives: The Classification of Educational Goals. Handbook II: The Affective Domain*, New York: David McKay.

Lawton, D. (1992) 'Whatever Happened to the TGAT Report?', in C. Gipps (ed.) *Developing Assessment for the National Curriculum*, London: Kogan Page.

Leighton, J. and Gierl, M.J. (2007) *Cognitive Diagnostic Assessment for Education: Theory and Applications*, New York: Cambridge University Press.

Van der Linden, W.J. and Glas, C.A.W. (eds) (2000) *Computerized Adaptive Testing: Theory and Practice,* Boston, MA: Kluwer.

MacLure, M. and Hargreaves, M. (1986) *Speaking and Listening. Assessment at Age 11*, an Assessment of Performance Unit report, Windsor: NFER-Nelson.

Mansell, W., James, M. and the Assessment Reform Group (2009), *Assessment in Schools. Fit for Purpose?*, a commentary by the Teaching and Learning Research Programme, London: Economic and Social Research Council.

Martin, M.O., Mullis, I.V.S., Beaton, A.E., Gonzales, E.J., Smith, T.A. and Kelly, D.L. (1997) *Science Achievement in the Primary School Years: IEA's Third International Mathematics and Science Study (TIMSS),* Chestnut Hill, MA: TIMSS International Study Centre, Boston College.

Martinez, J.F., Stecher, B. and Borko, H. (2009) 'Classroom assessment practices, teacher judgments, and student achievement in mathematics: evidence from the ECLS', *Educational Assessment*, 14: 78–102.

Mason, K. and Ruddock, G. (1986) *Decimals. Assessment at Age 11 and 15,* an Assessment of Performance Unit report, Windsor: NFER-Nelson.

Messick, S. (1989) 'Validity', in R. L. Linn (ed.) *Educational Measurement,* Washington, DC: American Council on Education/Macmillan Series on Higher Education.

Mons, N. and Pons, X., with van Zanten, A. and Pouille, J. (2010) *La Réception de Pisa en France. Connaissances et Régulation du Système Éducatif.* European Union. [Available in English translation]

Morgan, C. and Watson, A. (2002) 'The interpretive nature of teachers' assessment of students' mathematics: issues for equity', *Journal of Research in Mathematics Education*, 33: 78–110.

Morrison, H.G., Busch, J.C. and D'Arcy, J. (1994) 'Setting reliable national curriculum standards: A guide to the Angoff procedure', *Assessment in Education*, 1: 181–99.

Mullis, I.V.S., Martin, M.O., Beaton, A.E., Gonzales, E.J., Kelly, D.L. and Smith, T.A. (1997) *Mathematics Achievement in the Primary School Years: IEA's Third International Mathematics and Science Study (TIMSS),* Chestnut Hill, MA: TIMSS International Study Centre, Boston College.

Mullis, I. V. S., Martin, M. O., Gonzales, E. J. and Kennedy, A. M. (2003) *PIRLS 2001 International Report,* Boston: International Study Center.

Mullis, I. V. S., Martin, M. O. and Gonzales, E. J. (2004) *International Achievement in the Processes of Reading Comprehension: Results from PIRLS 2001 in 35 Countries*, Chestnut Hill, MA: Boston College.

Newton, P. (2009) 'The reliability of results from national curriculum testing in England', *Educational Research*, 51: 181–212.

Newton, P. (2010) 'Educational Assessment – Concepts and Issues: The Multiple Purposes of Assessment', in E. Baker, B. McGaw and P. Peterson (eds), *International Encyclopedia of Education. Third Edition,* Oxford: Elsevier.

Oates, T. (2010) *Could Do Better: Using International Comparisons to Refine the National Curriculum in England*, Cambridge: Cambridge Assessment.

Popham, W.J. (1997) 'Consequential validity: right concern – wrong concept', *Educational Measurement*, 16: 9–13.

Price, E., Powel, R. and Lloyd Griffiths, C. (1986) *Children Talking*, Cardiff: Welsh Office.

Purves, A.C. (1991) 'Brief History of IEA', in W.A. Hayes (ed.) *Activities, Institutions and People. IEA Guidebook 1991*, The Hague: The International Association for the Evaluation of Educational Achievement.

QCA (2007) *Level Threshold Tables and Age Standardised Scores for Key Stage 2 Tests in English, Mathematics and Science*, London: Qualifications and Curriculum Authority.

QCA (2008) *Early Years Foundation Stage Profile Handbook*, London: Qualifications and Curriculum Authority.

QCA (2009) *Research into Marking Quality: Studies to Inform Future Work of National Curriculum Assessment*, London: Qualifications and Curriculum Authority.

QCDA (2010a) *Key Stage 1 Assessment and Reporting Arrangements*, QCDA/10/5372, London: Qualifications and Curriculum Development Agency.

QCDA (2010b) *Technical and Methodological Statement for Key Stage 2 Science Sampling*, QCDA/10/4773, London: Qualifications and Curriculum Development Agency.

QCDA (2010c) *Science Sampling Arrangements. Key Stage 2 2010*, QCDA/10/4734, London: Qualifications and Curriculum Development Agency.

QCDA (2011a) *Calculating Overall Subject Levels*, QCDA/10/5369/p, London: Qualifications and Curriculum Development Agency.

QCDA (2011b) *English and Mathematics Test Administrators' Guide*, QCDA/11/5382/p, London: Qualifications and Curriculum Development Agency.

Reckase, M. D. (1989) 'Consequential validity from the test developer's perspective', *Educational Measurement*, 17: 13–16.

Reeves, D.J., Boyle, W.F. and Christie, T. (2001) 'The relationship between teacher assessments and pupil attainments in standard test tasks at key stage 2 1996–98', *British Educational Research Journal*, 27: 141–60.

Reynolds, C.R., Livingston, R.B. and Willson, V. (2008) *Measurement and Assessment*, Boston: Allyn & Bacon.

Ruddock, G., Sturman, L., Schagen, I., Styles, B., Gnaldi, M. and Vappula, H. (2004) *Where England Stands in the Trends in International Mathematics and Science Study (TIMSS) 2003: National Report for England*, Slough: NFER.

Russell, T., Black, P., Harlen, W., Johnson, S. and Palacio, D. (1988) *Science at Age 11. A Review of APU Survey Findings 1980–84*, London: HMSO.

Sainsbury, M. (1994) 'The Structure of National Curriculum Assessment', in D. Hutchison and I. Schagen (eds) *How Reliable is National Curriculum Assessment?*, Slough: NFER.

Sainsbury, M. and Sizmur, S. (1998) 'Level descriptions in the National Curriculum: what kind of criterion-referencing is this?', *Oxford Review of Education*, 24: 181–93.

Schofield, B., Bell, J., Black, P., Johnson, S., Murphy, P., Qualter, A. and Russell, T. (1989) *Science at Age 13. A Review of APU Survey Findings 1980–84*, London: HMSO.

Scottish Executive (2000) *Environmental Studies – Society, Science and Technology. 5–14 National Guidelines*, Revision of 1993 Guidelines, Edinburgh: Scottish Executive.

Scottish Government (2007) *Progress in International Reading Literacy Study (PIRLS) 2006. Highlights from Scotland's Results*, Edinburgh: The Scottish Government.

Scottish Government (2010a) *Curriculum for Excellence. Building the Curriculum 5, a Framework for Assessment: Executive Summary*, Edinburgh: Scottish Government.

Scottish Government (2010b) *2009 Scottish Survey of Achievement Reading and Writing*, Edinburgh: Scottish Government.

Scottish Government (2010c) *Programme for International Student Assessment (PISA) 2009 Highlights from Scotland's Results*, ISSN 1479-4569, Edinburgh: Scottish Government.

SCRE (1968) *Rising Standards in Scottish Primary Schools 1953–1963*. London: University of London Press for the Scottish Council for Research in Education.

Scriven, M. (1967) 'The Methodology of Evaluation', in R.W. Tyler, R.M. Gagne and M. Scriven (eds) *Perspectives of Curriculum Evaluation*, Chicago, IL: Rand McNally.

SEED (2002) *Programme for International Student Assessment. Scottish Report*, Edinburgh: Scottish Executive Education Department.

Shavelson, R.J., Baxter, G.P. and Pine, J. (1992) 'Performance assessments: political rhetoric and measurement reality', *Educational Researcher,* 21: 22–7.

Shavelson, R. and Webb, N. (1991) *Generalizability Theory: A Primer,* Newbury Park: CA: Sage.

Sizmur, S. and Sainsbury, M. (1997) 'Criterion referencing and the meaning of national curriculum assessment', *British Journal of Educational Studies,* 45: 123–40.

SOED (1991a) *Curriculum and Assessment in Scotland. National Guidelines. English Language 5–14,* Edinburgh: Scottish Office Education Department.

SOED (1991b) *Curriculum and Assessment in Scotland. National Guidelines. Mathematics 5–14,* Edinburgh: Scottish Office Education Department.

SOED (1993) *Curriculum and Assessment in Scotland. National Guidelines. Environmental Studies 5–14,* Edinburgh: Scottish Office Education Department.

SOEID (1999) *National Guidelines: Mathematics 5–14 Level F,* Edinburgh: Scottish Office Education and Industry Department.

Spooner, W. (2010) *The SEN Handbook for Trainee Teachers, NQTs and Teaching Assistants*, London: Routledge.

SQA (2009) *Guide to Assessment*, Glasgow: Scottish Qualifications Authority.

SSA (2006) *Scottish Survey of Achievement. 2005 English Language and Core Skills – Practitioner's Report*, Edinburgh: Scottish Executive.

Stanley, G., MacCann, R., Gardner, J., Reynolds, L. and Wild, I. (2009) *Review of Teacher Assessment: Evidence of What Works Best and Issues for Development,* Oxford: University of Oxford Centre for Educational Assessment.

Start, K.B. and Wells, B.K. (1972) *The Trend in Reading Standards,* Slough: NFER.

Stobart, G. (1991) 'GCSE meets key stage 4: something had to give', *Cambridge Journal of Education,* 21: 177–88.

Stobart, G. (2006) 'The Validity of Formative Assessment', in J. Gardner (ed.) *Assessment and Learning,* 133–46, London: Sage.

Stobart, G. (2008) *Testing Times. The Uses and Abuses of Assessment*, London: Routledge.

Stobart, G. (2009) 'Determining Validity in National Curriculum Assessments', *Educational Research,* 51: 161–79.

Strand, S. (2006) 'Comparing the predictive validity of reasoning tests and national end of key stage 2 tests: which tests are the "best"?', *British Educational Research Journal,* 32: 209–25.

Sturman, L., Ruddock, G., Burge, B., Styles, B., Lin, Y. and Vappula, H. (2008a) *England's Achievement in TIMSS 2007. National Report for England,* Slough: NFER.

Sturman, L., Ruddock, G., Burge, B., Styles, B., Lin, Y. and Vappula, H. (2008b) *England's Achievement in TIMSS 2007. Summary of the National Report for England,* Slough: NFER.

Swaffield, S. (ed.) (2008) *Unlocking Assessment*, Oxford: Routledge.

Taylor, W.L. (1953) 'Cloze procedure: a new tool for measuring readability', *Journalism Quarterly,* 30: 415–33.

TGAT (1988). *National Curriculum. Report of the Task Group on Assessment and Testing.* London: Department of Education and Science.

Thorpe, G. (2004) *Programme for International Student Assessment (PISA) 2003 Initial Report on Scotland's Performance in Mathematics, Science and Reading*, Edinburgh: Scottish Executive Education Department.

Tickell, C. (2011) *The Early Years: Foundations for Life, Health and Learning,* An Independent Report on the Early Years Foundation Stage to Her Majesty's Government.

Twist, L. and Sainsbury, M. (2009) 'Girl friendly? Investigating the gender gap in national reading tests at age 11', *Educational Research,* 51: 283–97.

Twist, L., Sainsbury, M., Woodthorpe, A. and Whetton, C. (2003) *Reading All Over the World: Progress in International Reading Literacy Study (PIRLS),* National Report for England, Slough: NFER.

Twist, L., Schagen, I. and Hodgson, C. (2007) *Readers and Reading: the National Report for England 2006,* PIRLS: Progress in International Reading Literacy Study, Slough: NFER.

Tymms, P. (2004) 'Are standards rising in English primary schools?', *British Educational Research Journal*, 30: 477–94.

Tymms, P. and Merrell, C. (2007) *Standards and Quality in English Primary Schools over Time: The National Evidence Research Survey* 4/1, London: Esmée Fairbairn Foundation.

Wainer, H. (ed.) (2000) *Computerized Adaptive Testing: A Primer,* (2nd Edition), Mahwah, NJ: Lawrence Erlbaum Associates.

Welford, G., Harlen, W. and Schofield, B. (1985) *Practical Testing Ages 11, 13 and 15*, an Assessment of Performance Unit report, London: Department of Education and Science.

Whetton, C. (2009) 'A brief history of a testing time: national curriculum assessment in England 1989–2008', *Educational Research*, 51: 137–59.

White, J. (1986) *The Assessment of Writing. Pupils Aged 11 and 15,* an Assessment of Performance Unit report, Slough: NFER-Nelson.

White, J. (1987) *Pupils' Attitudes to Writing*, an Assessment of Performance Unit report, Slough: NFER-Nelson.

White, J. and Welford, G. (1988) *The Language of Science*, an Assessment of Performance Unit report, London: Department of Education and Science.

Wiliam, D. (2001) 'Validity, reliability and all that jazz', *Education 3–13*, 29: 17–21.

Wilson, J.W. and Peaker, G.F. (eds) (1971) *International Study of Achievement in Mathematics* [Special issue]. *Journal for Research in Mathematics Education*, 2.

WJEC (2010). *Key Stages 2/3 Cluster Group External Moderation, Pilot 2010.* Cardiff: Welsh Joint Education Committee.

Wyatt-Smith, C. and Castleton, G. (2005) 'Examining how teachers judge student writing: An Australian case study', *Journal of Curriculum Studies*, 37: 131–54.

Wyse, D. and Torrance, H. (2009) 'The development and consequences of national curriculum assessment for primary education in England', *Educational Research*, 51: 213–28.

Author index

Subject index